DEATH AND VIOLENCE
ON THE RESERVATION

DEATH AND VIOLENCE ON THE RESERVATION

Homicide, Family Violence, and
Suicide in American Indian
Populations

RONET BACHMAN

Foreword by
MURRAY A. STRAUS

Auburn House _____

New York • Westport, Connecticut • London

Library of Congress Cataloging-in-Publication Data

Bachman, Ronet.
    Death and violence on the reservation : homicide, family violence,
and suicide in American Indian populations / Ronet Bachman ; foreword
by Murray A. Straus.
      p. cm.
    Includes bibliographical references and index.
    ISBN 0-86569-015-4 (alk. paper)
    1. Indians of North America—Crime. 2. Indians of North America—
Social conditions. 3. Violent crimes—United States. 4. Indians
of North America—Suicidal behavior.   I. Title.
E98.C87B33 1992
364.1'52'08997—dc20   91-37158

British Library Cataloguing in Publication Data is available.

Library of Congress Catalog Card Number: 91-37158
ISBN: 0-86569-015-4

First published in 1992

Auburn House, 88 Post Road West, Westport, CT 06881
An imprint of Greenwood Publishing Group, Inc.

Printed in the United States of America

The paper used in this book complies with the
Permanent Paper Standard issued by the National
Information Standards Organization (Z39.48-1984).

10 9 8 7 6 5 4 3 2 1

To Jan, my best friend and my mother

Contents

Figures and Tables

FIGURES

TABLES

Foreword

The fate of minority groups in American society is to have both their achievements and their problems ignored. That seems to be the case with violence among American Indians. The main exception occurs when those achievements or problems threaten Whites. Thus, there is great concern about violence among African Americans because it is perceived as a threat to Whites. One wonders what would happen to public concern about African American violence if the truth were widely known—that more than 90 percent of homicide victims are killed by those of their own race. Probably murder by African Americans would also be ignored, just as murder and other violence among American Indians is largely ignored by the public and scholars. Ronet Bachman's ground-breaking research is a major step in correcting that ignorance.

Death and Violence on the Reservation is also laudable in other ways. It is theoretically based; it interrelates three major types of violence, thereby increasing our understanding of each of them; and it combines the insight of qualitative data from her in-depth studies of American Indian victims and offenders with the precision of quantitative data from national surveys and national crime statistics.

Dr. Bachman's objectives are both scientific and humanitarian, and she has succeeded in both. Her findings enlarge our scientific understanding of violence among American Indians and of the social causes of this violence. These same findings also provide information that can assist in formulating steps to reduce the toll of violence among American Indians that is so starkly documented by Dr. Bachman's research.

Murray A. Straus
Co-Director, Family Research Laboratory
University of New Hampshire

Acknowledgments

The work involved in writing this book has spanned several years, and those I want to thank for their support, encouragement, and insightful suggestions are many. I acknowledge the support I received from a Postdoctoral Fellowship at the Family Research Laboratory, University of New Hampshire. The two years I spent there not only allowed me the time to write this book, but also provided me with one of the most supportive and inspiring environments in which to do so. For this I owe special thanks to the co-directors, Murray Straus and David Finkelhor. Others have also been instrumental in this work and in my professional development as a whole: Kirk Williams, who tirelessly provided critical suggestions for the homicide research I did; Arnold Linsky, who has been a calm, insightful, and meticulous mentor for the past six years; Larry Hamilton, who taught me the importance of responsible data analysis; Bud Khleif, who has assisted in my socialization as a qualitative researcher; Frederick Samuels, who has instilled in me the belief that as social scientists we must also strive to be humanists; Sally Ward, who has been there from the beginning as a model of honesty and fairness; John Harney, my editor, who by his faith in this work has given me motivation; and Meg Fergusson, my production editor, who has both meticulously and caringly guided this manuscript through its final stages. The points of view or opinions expressed herein are my own and do not represent the official position or policies of the U.S. Department of Justice.

Of course, this work could not have been possible without the balance and support of loving friends and colleagues. To the four kindred spirits in my life, Geri King, Barbara Wauchope, Dianne Cyr Carmody, and

Peggy Plass; to my source of creativity, Bruce Prehn; to my confidant, Alex Alvarez; and to my constant and everpresent source of support, Lori Williams—to all of you I say thanks.

My thanks also go to my parents, Ronald and Lois Bachman and Bill and Jan Vermilyea, who have instilled in me the passion and confidence necessary to produce this work.

I also want to acknowledge the person who, during the past two years, has provided me with infinite supplies of support, encouragement, insightful advice, caring criticism, laughter, and love: Ray Paternoster.

Perhaps most importantly, I want to thank the many individuals who have agreed to participate in this study. Each of you has been promised anonymity and so you will remain anonymous throughout this work. Your words and wisdom have added an invaluable glimpse of reality to the numbers presented in this book. I hope and pray that I have represented your words well. I will never forget you and the fact that you have *lived* the lives that I have written about.

DEATH AND VIOLENCE
ON THE RESERVATION

Chapter 1

Introduction

People are just beginning to understand the problems. We can't answer it for ourselves as a tribe. We need outside people to help us. That work is going to bridge our world with yours, our way of thinking with your way of thinking and we need that bridge. It's like a puzzle. And there's many pieces to that puzzle and they all can connect to each other. It's just that you need people with intelligence to say "Hey, let's put the puzzle down on the table and let's connect these pieces together. And let's build a story. And let's let the whole world hear that story. And it's a puzzle—a puzzle about people.

The above quote was taken from one of my first interviews with American Indian homicide offenders when I began my research on the etiology of American Indian homicide in 1987. For the past four years, these words have been a persistent source of motivation as I have explored this subject. The impetus for this search really had its origin in my childhood experiences. Having grown up on a ranch that was connected to an American Indian reservation in South Dakota, I witnessed the reality of reservation existence, where it was not unusual for an individual's life to be taken away or forever altered at a young age. Violence manifested itself in many ways and encompassed both acts of self-destruction, such as suicides and automobile accidents, and acts of aggression directed toward others.

When my research attention became focused on the etiology of violence, I was struck by a glaring gap in the literature. Studies examining the causes of American Indian crime and violence, and particularly research that used multivariate statistical techniques, was virtually nonexistent. This perception of a gap in the literature was validated by a glance through practically every introductory criminology textbook. Crime and Blacks and crime and Hispanics were often addressed, but American Indian criminality was absent. This absence existed alongside descriptive statistics that revealed arrest rates for American Indians to be far higher than those for either Blacks or Whites. The number of deaths resulting from acts of violence was also known to be higher (Stewart, 1964; Reasons, 1972; Jensen, Straus, and Harris, 1977; Levy and Konitz, 1969, 1971, 1974; May, 1975, 1982a, 1982b).

Given the apparent prevalence of violent death among American Indian populations, coupled with the relative lack of research attention by criminologists, the need for a more comprehensive comparative study seemed great. This need was the catalyst for the present work. This book examines three forms of violence in American Indian populations: homicide, spousal assault, and suicide. These forms of violence were selected because they have each been identified by many tribes and American Indian communities as serious problems in need of attention.

Homicide and spousal assault are both acts of aggression directed outward, with homicide representing the most extreme form of this outward aggression. Suicide is an aggressive behavior that represents the most extreme form of aggression directed inward. While self- and other-directed acts of aggression represent two different manifestations of violence, each contains components of frustration that are released in an aggressive manner. Consequently, each can be subsumed under the definition of violence offered by Lane (1979). According to Lane, violence is defined as physically reckless, aggressive, or destructive behavior. Similarly, for purposes of this book, violence will be defined as physically reckless, aggressive, or destructive behavior that is intended to injure the self or another.

The purpose of this book is to provide a systematic and detailed examination of homicide, family violence, and suicide in contemporary American Indian society. Because there is a paucity of research in the area of American Indian crime, this work has the dual purpose of providing an epidemiological assessment of the extent of this violence while also providing a theoretical grounding for the study of violence in American Indian populations. The research presented here is sociological in its focus. It examines the social structural factors that are related to the incidence of this violence. After estimating incidence and prevalence rates for each of these forms of violence, this book will move on to examine the causes and correlates of each. Before proceeding, however, it is important to define exactly what is meant by the term *American Indian*.

WHO IS AN AMERICAN INDIAN?

It is an almost impossible task to describe American Indians as a group because not everyone agrees on just *who* is an American Indian. According to the federal government's Bureau of Indian Affairs (BIA), an American Indian is legally defined as a person who is an enrolled or registered member of a tribe or whose blood quantum is one-fourth or more, genealogically derived. This level varies, however, with some tribes setting their blood quantum requirements much lower and some setting them higher.

The U.S. Bureau of the Census does not use the BIA criteria, but relies on self-identification. According to the U.S. Census (1980), there are over 1.5 million American Indian people in the United States, including Aleuts, Native Alaskans, and Inuits. This number represents all people who classify themselves as American Indians. This classification procedure is problematic, however, in that it is a social-legal, not a biological, classification. For example, many people who self-classify themselves as Indian or who enjoy the legal privileges granted to American Indians (i.e., those on tribal rolls) are, in fact, of mixed ancestry.

The number of people who self-identify themselves as American Indian is increasing at an unprecedented rate, according to both the 1980 and the 1990 U.S. Census counts. Let me give an example. In a projection of the 1980 American Indian population made in 1979 (assuming annual growth of 2.55 percent), the Indian Health Service *underestimated* the actual 1980 Census count by 17 percent. In fact, the 1980 Census count was an approximately 71 percent increase over the 1970 recorded total of American Indians. Some posit that the increase between the 1970 and 1980 Census reports is the product of an overcount in 1980 due to changes in the way in which the Census Bureau counts American Indians (*New York Times*, March 5, 1991, p. 1). That is, since 1950, the Bureau has increasingly relied on respondents' self-identification of race and ethnic identity in these counts. One writer states, "The data from these more recent enumerations [1980 Census] suggests that a significant number of individuals who in the past identified with other races, have increasingly begun to view themselves as American Indian, at least for Census recording purposes" (Green, 1988, p. 4).

According to the *New York Times*, Census officials in 1990 are once again finding a dramatic increase in the number of people who identify themselves as American Indians. In fact, every state for which counts by racial groups have been reported to date has had an increase in the number of self-identified American Indians. Table 1.1 lists both 1980 and 1990 Census Bureau counts of American Indians and the percentage increase of this population between these two counts. One state, Alabama, reports an increase in its American Indian population of over 100 percent.

Table 1.1
Census Bureau Counts of the American Indian Population
for 1980 and 1990

STATE	American Indian Pop. in 1980	American Indian Pop. in 1990	1980–1990 Percent Increase
Alabama	7,583	16,506	117.7%
Arizona	152,745	203,527	33.2
Arkansas	9,428	12,773	35.5
California	201,369	242,184	20.3
Connecticut	4,553	6,654	46.8
Delaware	1,328	2,019	52.0
Dist. of Columbia	1,031	1,466	42.2
Georgia	7,616	13,348	75.3
Hawaii	2,768	5,099	84.2
Illinois	16,283	21,836	34.1
Indiana	7,836	12,720	62.3
Iowa	5,455	7,349	34.7
Kansas	15,373	21,965	42.9
Kentucky	3,610	5,769	59.8
Louisiana	12,085	18,541	53.7
Maryland	8,021	12,972	61.7
Michigan	40,050	55,638	38.9
Minnesota	35,016	49,909	42.5
Mississippi	6,180	8,525	37.9
Missouri	12,321	19,835	61.0
Montana	37,270	47,679	27.9
Nebraska	9,195	12,410	35.0
Nevada	13,308	19,637	47.5
New Hampshire	1,352	2,134	57.8
New Jersey	8,394	14,970	78.3
New York	39,582	62,651	58.3
North Carolina	64,652	80,155	24.0
North Dakota	20,158	25,917	28.6
Ohio	12,239	20,358	66.3
Oklahoma	169,459	252,420	49.0
Oregon	27,314	38,498	40.9
Pennsylvania	9,465	14,733	55.7
Rhode Island	2,898	4,071	40.5
South Dakota	44,968	50,573	12.5
Texas	40,075	65,877	64.4
Vermont	984	1,696	72.4
Virginia	9,454	14,282	61.6
Wisconsin	29,499	39,387	33.5
Wyoming	7,094	9,479	33.6

Note: These are population counts reported by states to the Census Bureau as of March 30, 1991.

The *New York Times* reports, "As American society becomes more accepting and admiring of the Indian heritage, and as governments set aside contracts and benefits for tribe members, an increasing number of Indians feel freer to assert their identities" (March 5, 1991, p. 1). Because the Census Bureau does not require proof of heritage, it is impossible to know how many people falsely assert an Indian background. To be sure, there has been a positive change in attitudes toward American Indians, which has perhaps led to an increase in the number of people who identify or "want to identify" themselves as Indians. This is certainly reflected in recent media attention paid to Indians, as in the case of the box office hit *Dances with Wolves*.

I concentrate on this problem because it has important implications for the homicide and suicide rates that were generated for this research. For example, if one adheres to the notion that there is an overcount in the 1980 Census, the homicide rates that were calculated (at the national, state, and reservation levels) could be biased downward relative to any rates that may have been calculated prior to the 1980 Census. This would occur because of inflated denominators. The extent of bias, of course, is unknown, and the implications of this should not be lost.

The next issue that must be addressed is the cultural diversity that exists among tribal units. The American Indian population is extremely varied. The Bureau of Indian Affairs recognizes 505 tribes in the United States, including 197 Alaska Native village groups in Alaska. Today, approximately one-half of American Indians live on reservations, and an equal number live in urban areas. There are about 304 federal Indian reservations in the United States. The largest of these, the Navajo Reservation, includes almost 16 million acres of land in Arizona, New Mexico, and Utah, but many reservations are less than 1,000 acres. Reservation land may also be owned and occupied by non-Indians.

The label "American Indian" undoubtedly evokes many images for most of us. For some, the image is romanticized with a positive mystique; for others, it is a denigrated image of people devoid of social discipline, violent by nature, and perceived to have problems with alcohol. But American Indians fit neither of these stereotypes. Some live according to their traditions, some receive welfare, and others earn a living as farmers, ranchers, factory workers, or professionals.

A major variable contributing to this cultural diversity is the degree to which an individual either accepts traditionalism or becomes acculturated to mainstream society. The continuum stretches from the very traditional Indian who was born on a reservation and speaks the tribal language to the Indian who was born in a city, speaks English, and feels little identification with a tribe.

This heterogeneity exists even within a single reservation. For example, Riner (1979) examined 174 households on the Blackfoot, Sioux, and Navajo reservations and was able to distinguish four types of households: The *isolated family*, located in a remote area of a reservation with a strong preference for use of the native language; the *traditional family*, generally bilingual and actively participating in tribal ceremonies; the *bicultural family*, living on a reservation and engaging in traditional ceremonies, but preferring to speak English; and the *acculturated family*, speaking English as the primary language and engaging in family activities that approximate White norms. Given this diversity, one must be careful to avoid stereotyping based on general assumptions.

The term *American Indian* as used in this book broadly refers to all persons of Indian, Eskimo, or Aleut descent. It does not take into account the diversity that exists among tribes. However, along with the heterogeneity that exists within the population of American Indians, all tribes share some values and experiences. Since the beginning of European contact, all tribes have similarly experienced economic and social disruptions of their communities, of their traditional family life, and of their respective roles in community affairs. These experiences have produced a unification among many tribal groups and have led to the current Pan-Indian movement. In fact, Dr. Robert Thomas (1990), a professor of anthropology at the University of Arizona, who is also Cherokee, writes, "In some sense, Indian tribes are becoming collections of generalized tribal personalities without a truly native institutional structure nor a coherent culture, tradition, and language" (p. 53).

Although this unification does exist among most tribal groups, it should be reiterated that considerable diversity can still be found in the American Indian population. As used here, the term *American Indian* does not distinguish among the culturally and legally differing tribes living in this country. Thus, the findings reported in this book may exhibit unique variations at local tribal levels.

SOCIAL CHARACTERISTICS OF AMERICAN INDIANS TODAY

The social characteristics of the American Indian population will be discussed in greater detail in later chapters. However, the purpose of this section is to briefly familiarize the reader with the structural world in which many American Indians live. As is the case with cultural variations among American Indian tribes, great diversity in such things as income and employment also exists. But when talking about poverty, social statistics that denote averages can be very illuminating. In fact, some statistical averages show that American Indians in this country suffer the entire range of deleterious conditions that are present in most Third World countries. Let me give you some examples.

Perhaps statistics on life expectancy are the best testimonial to the harshness and deprivation that many American Indians must endure. The average life span of the American Indian is about eight to ten years below the national average. Premature death occurs in many forms. The maternal mortality rate for American Indians is around 11 per 100,000 live births. This rate is approximately 40 percent higher than the U.S. average maternal mortality rate. While the infant mortality rate for American Indians has decreased by approximately 85 percent since the 1950s, infant deaths still average a rate of 11 for every 1,000 live births. Further, the postneonatal death rate, which records infant deaths that occur from 28 days to 11 months after birth, is approximately 40 percent higher for American Indians than the U.S. population in general.

If an American Indian lives beyond one year of age, the probability that he or she will die prematurely from other causes is also higher than it is for the U.S. population as a whole. For example, the Indian Health Service and Centers for Disease Control estimate that Indian deaths from motor vehicle accidents are more than three times higher than the national average. Deaths from alcoholism are almost six times higher, with deaths specifically caused by chronic liver disease and cirrhosis averaging five to six times higher than the U.S. averages. Death rates from pneumonia and influenza are more than double the national rates, and deaths from tuberculosis are nearly four times as high. And as we will see in the chapters that follow, death rates from homicide and suicide are almost double the national averages and can be as much as eight times higher in some reservation communities.

Social and economic characteristics on average still lag behind those of the population in general. From 50 to 60 percent of all American Indian children drop out of school before completing the twelfth grade, compared to only 20 to 25 percent of all other races combined. Unemployment averages around 50 percent, with some reservations experiencing unemployment rates as high as 80 to 90 percent. Nearly one of every four American Indian families has an income below the poverty level. Let me illustrate this another way. In 1979, half of all Indian families had an annual income of less than $14,000. During that same year, half of all White families in the United States had an annual income of almost $21,000 (Snipp and Summers, 1991).

In addition, one of the most visible signs of deprivation in reservation communities is reservation housing. Again, although living conditions vary considerably, running water, central heating, indoor plumbing, and electricity are not always present. In fact, approximately 20 to 30 percent of housing in some reservation communities lacks both indoor plumbing and electricity. While many of these conditions appear to be getting better, many seem to be getting worse. The reasons for the further decline in health and economic conditions are varied and will be discussed in later chapters (see particularly Chapter 8). While a more detailed breakdown of these average characteristics would reveal conditions far worse on some tribal levels, these national averages are quite revealing indicators of the harsh reality that many American Indians live with.

THE METHODOLOGY USED IN THIS BOOK

Social scientists, for the most part, can be divided into two broad methodological camps: those who advocate the use of quantitative methods and those who advocate the use of qualitative methods. Proponents of quantitative methods see formal statistical hypothesis testing as the only road to rigorous science. According to this extreme, we can acquire objective knowledge of social life only through classifying, measuring, tabulating, and using statistical methods.

At the other extreme, defenders of qualitative research argue that most of what really matters in any real-world situation is nonquantifiable. In fact, the radical qualitative perspective holds that quantitative methods impose a structure and a form inherently alien to the texture of social life, which can be grasped only in its complex detail and wholeness. Statistics might be useful to organize superficial facts wanted for administrative purposes, but they reveal nothing about the basic nature of social life. Because of this, the notion of quantitative methods is, at best, mischievous (Wilson, 1986).

Fielding and Fielding (1986) have satirized this debate succinctly in the following quote: "The caricature of qualitative research is that it is soft whereas quantitative research is hard; qualitative researchers call quantitative researchers 'number-crunchers' and the riposte of the latter is that the former are mere 'navel-gazers.' "

The division of social research into these quantitative and qualitative domains seems to have led to a state of affairs in which, unfortunately, proponents of each seem oblivious to the other's merits. In reality, all research is equally vulnerable to bias, emotion, laxity, logical error, and even fraud. Both qualitative and quantitative methods have strengths and weaknesses. For example, the scientific ideas associated with quantitative methods include rigid experimental control, reliable and valid test instruments, probability sampling, and rigorous statistical analysis of data. There also exists one major disadvantage: an outcome that cannot be quantified reliably cannot be investigated. For this reason, many favor qualitative methods. Here the goal is to reconstruct imaginatively the standpoint or perspective of the people being studied—to give their behavior meaning. The strength of this methodology is the depth of insight it permits. Its weakness, however, is that reliability and validity are difficult to assess.

Although there have been attempts to show how both approaches complement each other, most authors who have documented this pseudo-debate believe a fault line still exists within our discipline. As Zelditch (1962) has stated, "Quantitative data are often thought of as hard and qualitative as real and deep; thus if you prefer hard data you are for quantification and if you prefer real and deep data you are for qualitative participant observation. What to do if you prefer data that are real, deep and hard is not immediately apparent'' (p. 566).

This dilemma poses a problem for many researchers, including myself. In the research I conducted for this book, I adopted both methods of inquiry. This multiple method approach has been called *triangulation*, a term that derives from surveying. Let me give an example. Knowing a single landmark only locates one somewhere along a line in a single direction from the landmark. However, with two landmarks, one can take bearings on both and locate oneself at their intersection (Fielding and Fielding, 1986). In research, methodological triangulation involves combining different methods in the same project to reveal different dimensions of the same phenomenon.

With each of the acts of violence explored in this book (homicide, domestic violence, and suicide), I conducted both in-depth interviews and statistical analyses of aggregate-level data. This methodology proved invaluable. The qualitative fieldwork I conducted assisted my subsequent quantitative analyses by providing a theoretical framework from which to start. It also allowed me to add meaning and depth to the statistical relationships that were found at the aggregate level. In a sense, this methodology also provided validity to the conclusions drawn. For example, social disorganization and economic deprivation were found to be significant predictors of homicide both at the aggregate level (the state and reservation levels) and at the individual level (among the homicide offenders I interviewed). Campbell and Fiske (1959) state:

If a hypothesis can survive the confrontation of a series of complementary methods of testing, it contains a degree of validity unattainable by one tested within the more constricted framework of a single method. . . . Findings from this latter approach must always be subject to the suspicion that they are method-bound: Will the comparison totter when exposed to an equally prudent but diffrent testing method? (p. 82)

In using this triangulated methodology, it was my goal to make the findings of this research more cumulative and unequivocal, while at the same time more adequately controlling the bias that I, as a researcher, may have brought along with me.

SCOPE OF THE BOOK

The book begins with an analysis of American Indian homicide. Chapter 2 performs an extensive comparative analysis of American Indian, White and Black homicide rates at the national level. This chapter examines rates of homicide disaggregated by the victim/offender relationship (family, acquaintance, stranger), precipitating circumstance of the homicide (felony, robbery, suspected felony, conflict, nonfelony), weapon type (handgun, other gun, knife, blunt object), and gender (male, female). Homicide rates are also presented by state and region. The chapter concludes with an examination of homicide and suicide rates and how they relate to each other for all three racial/ethnic groups for the time period 1965-1983.

Chapter 3 begins examining the etiology of American Indian homicide by presenting an analysis of homicide offender interviews. It explores the social contributors of American Indian homicide. From this analysis, a theoretical model of American Indian homicide is delineated that includes elements of social disorganization, economic deprivation, a subculture of violence, and culture conflict and perceived powerlessness, as well as an intervening variable—alcohol/drug abuse. Also included in the model is the antecedent variable of internal colonialism. By identifying these sensitizing concepts, the statistical analysis presented in the following chapter is more responsibly informed. Chapter 4 estimates statistical models predicting American Indian homicide at the reservation and state levels. The investigation of American Indian homicide concludes in Chapter 5 with a discussion of alternative explanations, including a discussion of the discriminatory imposition of the law and medical resource availability.

Chapter 6 examines the second form of other-directed violence covered in this book: violence in American Indian families. The chapter combines both qualitative fieldwork data that were obtained at three battered women's shelters located on reservations and a quantitative analysis of data obtained from the 1985 National Family Violence Survey. After estimating incidence and prevalence rates of spousal assault in American Indian families, the chapter explores some contributing factors of this violence, including stress and alcohol abuse.

In Chapter 7, we move our inquiry to the act of violence that represents the most extreme form of aggression directed inward: suicide. This chapter relies almost exclusively on data obtained from the Indian Health Service for the period 1980-1987. After a brief qualitative account of the reality of suicide in Indian communities, the chapter focuses on a statistical analysis of the causes and contributors to American Indian suicide at the reservation level.

Chapter 2

Trends in American Indian Homicide

How common is homicide in the American Indian population? How does the American Indian homicide rate differ from homicide rates for Whites and Blacks? This chapter will answer these questions by investigating national incidence rates and trends of homicide for American Indians, Blacks and Whites. This chapter gives the reader a general overview of what relationships and precipitating circumstances characterize American Indian homicide at the national level. Before examining national incidence rates, however, it is first important to define exactly what homicide means for the purposes of this chapter.

Homicide is the killing of one human being by another without legal justification or excuse. As a legal category, homicide can be criminal or noncriminal. Criminal homicide is generally referred to as first-degree murder when one person causes the death of another with premeditation and intent. It is usually considered second-degree murder when death is caused with malice and intent, but without premeditation. Voluntary manslaughter involves intent to inflict bodily injury, but without deliberate intent to kill, whereas involuntary manslaughter is reckless or negligent killing without intent to harm. Noncriminal homicide includes excusable homicide, which occurs primarily in cases of self-defense, and justifiable homicide (e.g., the killing of an individual by a police officer in the line of duty) (Uniform Crime Reports, 1990).

Anyone who attempts an empirical analysis of homicide faces operational difficulty simply because there is a great variety of situations and motives behind aggregate homicide rates. The situations range from brutal killings that occur in the course of a trivial quarrel and crimes of passion to premeditated and skillfully planned murders. Further, what about an assault victim who survives simply because he or she had quick access to medical resources, whereas another dies because of inadequate medical attention? From this point of view, the legal distinction between attempted and completed homicide is difficult to defend because the victim's survival is often the result of chance, and this almost certainly has an effect on criminal homicide statistics.

With the above caveats in mind, for purposes of this book, homicide will be defined as incidents of murder and nonnegligent manslaughter. Specifically, the homicide data analyzed in this chapter were obtained from the Supplementary Homicide Report collected by the Federal Bureau of Investigation as a part of its Uniform Crime Reporting program. The entire data set was compiled at the University of New Hampshire and is referred to as the Comparative Homicide File (CHF) (Williams & Flewelling, 1987, 1988). Among these incidents of homicide, the sample is restricted to one-on-one cases and covers the entire 1980-1984 period, not individual years. This averaging procedure was used to reduce the influence of random aberrations in year-to-year estimates, in addition to the possible unreliability of rates based on low frequencies. Using weighting and adjustment procedures for missing data, the total homicide rates were calculated as follows:

$$\text{Homicide rate} = [(I/P) \times 100,000]/5$$

where I = the total number of weighted and adjusted race-specific (American Indian, Black, White) incidents of murder and nonnegligent manslaughter and P = the total race-specific population. The division by five indicates that the rates are calculated over the 1980-1984 period and then expressed on a per-year bias. For a detailed description of the rate calculation procedure, see Williams and Flewelling (1987).

INCIDENCE

Table 2.1 displays average disaggregated homicide rates for American Indians, Blacks, and Whites for the years 1980-1984. The racial/ethnic differentials that exist among these categories are more easily discernible graphically and are presented in Figures 2.1 to 2.5. From Figure 2.1 it can be seen that Blacks had the highest total homicide rate of any group during this time period (33.1 per 100,000 population) compared to 9.6 and 4.6 for American Indians and Whites, respectively. Although Blacks maintained the highest rate, it is important to note that American Indian homicides are more than two times higher than those of Whites. This rate differential persists when rates are further disaggregated by weapon, victim/offender relationship, precipitating circumstance, and gender.

Table 2.1
Homicide Rates per 100,000 by Weapon, Relationship of Victim and Offender, Gender, and Circumstance, 1980-1984

Homicide Type	AMER.IND.	BLACK	WHITE
		RACE/ETHNICITY	
HANDGUN	2.4 (26.1%)	15.1 (50.1%)	2.0 (40.8%)
OTHGUN	1.8 (19.5%)	4.2 (13.9%)	0.8 (16.3%)
KNIVES	2.7 (29.3%)	6.8 (22.5%)	1.0 (20.4%)
BLUNT OBJ	1.4 (15.2%)	2.6 (8.6%)	0.7 (14.2%)
OTHWEAP	0.9 (9.7%)	1.4 (4.4%)	0.4 (8.1%)
	(100%)	(100%)	(100%)
FAMILY	2.1 (23.3%)	6.3 (21.3%)	1.3 (26.0%)
ACQUAINTANCE	5.4 (60.0%)	17.1 (57.8%)	2.3 (46.0%)
STRANGER	1.5 (16.7%)	6.2 (20.9%)	1.4 (28.0%)
	(100%)	(100%)	(100%)
MALE	40.9 (85.6%)	58.2 (84.7%)	8.5 (89.4%)
FEMALE	6.9 (14.4%)	10.5 (15.2%)	1.0 (10.5%)
	(100%)	(100%)	(100%)
FELONY	0.4 (3.3%)	0.7 (2.3%)	0.2 (4.1%)
ROBBERY	0.9 (7.5%)	1.9 (6.3%)	0.5 (10.4%)
SUSP.FELONY	0.5 (4.2%)	1.1 (3.6%)	0.2 (4.1%)
CONFLICT	6.1 (51.2%)	15.8 (52.4%)	2.0 (41.6%)
NONFELONY			
Vice, Gang, etc.	2.1 (17.6%)	4.8 (15.9%)	0.9 (18.7%)
UNDETERMINED	1.9 (15.9%)	5.8 (19.2%)	1.0 (20.8%)
	(100%)	(100%)	(100%)
TOTAL RATE	9.6	33.1	4.6

Note: Each category of disaggregated homicide rates (i.e., weapon specific, relationship specific, total, etc.) was calculated independently. Because of weighting and adjustment procedures, each category total does not equal the total rate for each racial/ethnic group.

Weapon-Specific Rates

Weapon-specific homicide rates by racial/ethnic identity are displayed in Figure 2.2. A larger percentage of Black (50 percent) and White (41 percent) homicide offenders used a handgun, compared to the percentage of American Indians who killed with a handgun (26 percent). The weapon most frequently used by American Indians is the knife, which

Figure 2.1
Total Homicide Rates, 1980-1984

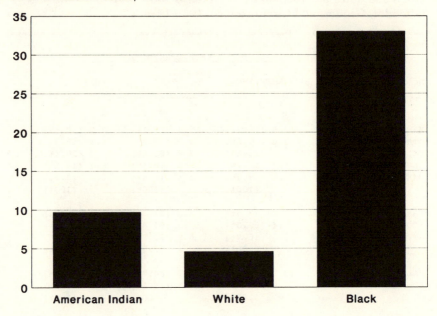

Figure 2.2
Weapon Specific Homicide Rates, 1980-1984

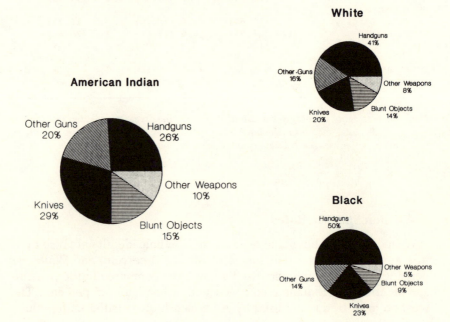

characterized 29 percent of all homicide deaths. Homicides resulting from other guns (i.e., long and shoulder guns) were also more frequent among the American Indian population (20 percent) than among either the Black (14 percent) or White (16 percent) population. The percentage of American Indian homicides resulting from the use of blunt objects was also higher than the equivalent percentages for Blacks and Whites. Perhaps the greater frequency of these knife and blunt object homicides among the Indian population is due to the availability of these objects at a relatively low cost.

Victim/Offender Relationship Rates

Victim/offender-relationship-specific homicides are displayed in Figure 2.3. Although more homicide victims were acquaintances than either family members or strangers in all racial/ethnic groups, American Indian victims had a higher probability of being acquaintances (60 percent) than did either Black (58 percent) or White (46 percent) victims. American Indians killed proportionately fewer strangers (17 percent) than did either Black (21 percent) or White (28 percent) offenders. Further, the percentage of White stranger homicides was higher than either the Black or Indian stranger rate. This was true of the percentage of White family homicides as well.

Figure 2.3
Victim/Offender Relationship Specific Homicide Rates, 1980-1984

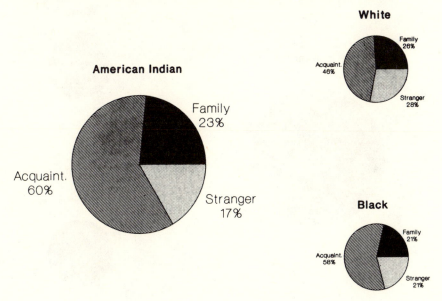

This higher proportion of acquaintance homicides in the American Indian population is partially explainable by the rurality of most reservation settings. Reservations are usually relatively small and often isolated. In this environment, most of the residents know everyone in the population. Thus, there may be more opportunity for the occurrence of acquaintance homicides compared to those perpetrated by strangers. As approximately half of all Indians live in reservation settings, this may be one explanation for the highr proportion of acquaintance homicides in the American Indian national rate.

Gender-Specific Rates

The gender-specific homicide rates are graphically presented in Figure 2.4. Although homicide appears to be a predominantly male phenomenon for each racial/ethnic group, some interesting trends emerge. Females in both American Indian (14 percent) and Black (15 percent) groups commit proportionately more homicides than do White (11 percent) females. Both American Indian and Black females commit a similar proportion of homicides, but the female-perpetrated homicide rate for Whites is much lower.

Figure 2.4
Gender Specific Homicide Rates, 1980-1984

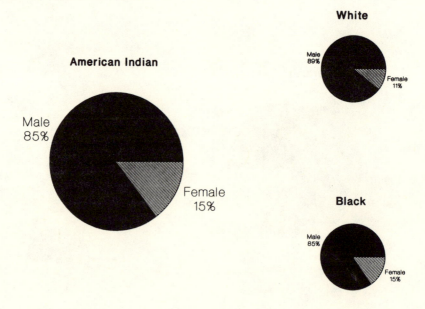

Circumstance-Specific Rates

Figure 2.5 displays the circumstance-specific homicide rates by race/ethnicity. Overall, a glance across all racial/ethnic groups gives a similar picture of homicide by circumstance. Most homicide victims, regardless of race or ethnicity, are killed in conflict situations (e.g., arguments). Both Indian and Black conflict homicides are proportionately similar (61 and 65 percent, respectively), while White conflict homicides represent a much smaller proportion (53 percent) of all homicides classified by these circumstance categories. White homicides are also characterized by proportionately more felony and robbery homicides than are either Indian or Black homicides. American Indians, however, have a slightly higher proportion of felony and robbery homicides than do Blacks.

State and Regional Variation in Homicide

Table 2.2 displays regional patterns of homicide by race and ethnicity for four regions of the United States: North East, North Central, South, and West. Table 2.3 illustrates regional variations of homicide, using a

Figure 2.5
Circumstance Specific Homicide Rates, 1980-1984

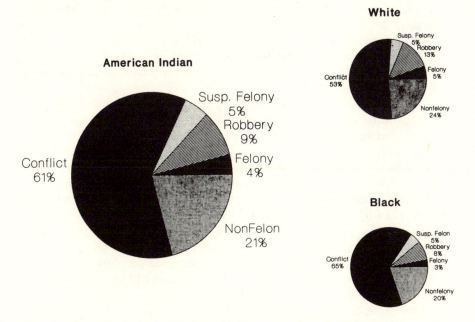

Note: Percentages exclude the "Undetermined" category presented in Table 2.1.

more detailed breakdown of nine regions. It is clear that the risk of homicide varies among the different regions of the country depending on one's racial/ethnic identity.

In general, the highest rate of homicide for the total population occurs in the South. But this is somewhat misleading. When disaggregated by race, the West generally has the highest homicide rates for all three racial/ethnic groups. Homicide patterns are somewhat similar for both American Indians and Blacks, as each group exhibits the highest homicide rates in the West and North Central regions of the country, whereas White homicide rates are highest in the West and the South. Focusing on American Indian homicide rates, it appears that the North Central (11.87) and West (11.72) regions have approximately equal homicide rates, while the North East (4.87) and South (4.83) have much lower rates. When the country is broken down in greater detail, we see from Table 2.3 that the Pacific region has the highest mean American Indian homicide rate (18.48), followed by the West North Central region (14.89).

SUMMARY

This chapter has described national and regional patterns of homicide in American Indian, Black, and White racial/ethnic groups. While Blacks have the highest total homicide rate of any group, American Indians have a homicide rate that is more than double that of Whites. It should be noted here that the national rate of American Indian homicide is slightly deceiving. It will be seen in Chapter 4 that American Indian homicide rates at the state and reservation county levels sometimes reach astronomical levels. Some reservation counties have American Indian homicide rates over 100 per 100,000 population (e.g., Harney, Oregon: 127 per 100,000).

When the total homicide rate at the national level was disaggregated, the patterns of homicide among the three racial/ethnic groups were somewhat similar. Although American Indian homicide was characterized by a higher proportion of knife homicides than was either White or Black homicide, all racial/ethnic group homicides were characterized by a high proportion of firearm deaths. If both handgun and other gun (shoulder guns, etc.) percentages are combined, 46 percent of Indian, 64 percent of Black, and 57 percent of White homicide offenders used firearms in the 1980-1984 period. The highest proportion of circumstance-specific homicides fell into the conflict category across all racial/ethnic groups. Although the majority of homicides were perpetrated by males, both American Indian and Black females committed proportionately more homicides than did White females.

One troubling question arises from this analysis: Why are national rates of American Indian homicide not higher than they are? Given that

Table 2.2
American Indian, Black, White, and Total Homicide Offender
Rates for Four Regions of the United States, 1980-1984

==

A. AMERICAN INDIAN TOTAL OFFENDER RATES

	Mean	Std Dev	States
U.S. A.I. Total	8.2560	8.5180	51
NORTH EAST	4.8787	4.2566	9
NORTH CENTRAL	11.8719	9.3806	12
SOUTH	4.8388	5.2359	17
WEST	11.7249	11.0368	13

B. BLACK TOTAL OFFENDER RATES

	Mean	Std Dev	States
U.S. Black Total	29.8261	11.8466	51
NORTH EAST	25.7869	7.9669	9
NORTH CENTRAL	29.0775	12.4881	12
SOUTH	28.1201	8.3303	17
WEST	35.5445	15.9567	13

C. WHITE TOTAL OFFENDER RATES

	Mean	Std Dev	States
U.S. White Total	4.1928	2.4911	51
NORTH EAST	2.6850	1.1333	9
NORTH CENTRAL	2.2833	1.1540	12
SOUTH	5.2074	2.0484	17
WEST	5.6725	3.0005	13

D. TOTAL POPULATION OFFENDER RATES

	Mean	Std Dev	States
U.S. Total	6.8061	4.8271	51
NORTH EAST	3.9906	2.3928	9
NORTH CENTRAL	4.2703	2.8041	12
SOUTH	10.3781	5.6925	17
WEST	6.4250	3.4997	13

Table 2.3
Homicide Offender Rates by Race/Ethnicity for Nine Census Divisions, 1980-1984

==

A. AMERICAN INDIAN TOTAL OFFENDER RATES

	Mean	Std Dev	States
U.S. American Indian Total	8.2560	8.5180	51
NEW ENGLAND	3.4344	4.5357	6
MIDDLE ATLANTIC	7.7672	1.5057	3
EAST NORTH CENTRAL	7.6404	9.2108	5
WEST NORTH CENTRAL	14.8945	8.8987	7
SOUTH ATLANTIC	6.2473	6.5284	9
EAST SOUTH CENTRAL	3.2289	2.2440	4
WEST SOUTH CENTRAL	3.2795	3.8564	4
MOUNTAIN	7.5008	2.2819	8
PACIFIC	18.4835	16.2339	5

B. BLACK TOTAL OFFENDER RATES

	Mean	Std Dev	States
U.S. Black Total	29.8261	11.8466	51
NEW ENGLAND	23.7813	7.9714	6
MIDDLE ATLANTIC	29.7981	7.6697	3
EAST NORTH CENTRAL	33.4974	9.1868	5
WEST NORTH CENTRAL	25.9204	14.2035	7
SOUTH ATLANTIC	26.0704	9.7036	9
EAST SOUTH CENTRAL	27.2881	1.4435	4
WEST SOUTH CENTRAL	33.5640	7.9926	4
MOUNTAIN	36.2602	16.5547	8
PACIFIC	34.3995	16.7803	5

Table 2.3 (Continued)

==

A. WHITE OFFENDER TOTAL RATES

	Mean	Std Dev	States
U.S. White Total	4.1928	2.4911	51
NEW ENGLAND	2.2552	.3409	6
MIDDLE ATLANTIC	3.5444	1.7847	3
EAST NORTH CENTRAL	2.8013	.6831	5
WEST NORTH CENTRAL	1.9133	1.3217	7
SOUTH ATLANTIC	4.7754	1.6145	9
EAST SOUTH CENTRAL	4.6551	1.0570	4
WEST SOUTH CENTRAL	6.7314	3.2011	4
MOUNTAIN	5.8999	3.4616	8
PACIFIC	5.3086	2.4019	5

D. TOTAL POPULATION OFFENDER RATES

	Mean	Std Dev	States
U.S. Total	6.8061	4.8271	51
NEW ENGLAND	2.7408	.8236	6
MIDDLE ATLANTIC	6.4902	2.6737	3
EAST NORTH CENTRAL	6.0131	2.3421	5
WEST NORTH CENTRAL	3.0255	2.5275	7
SOUTH ATLANTIC	10.6593	7.6313	9
EAST SOUTH CENTRAL	9.3579	1.6412	4
WEST SOUTH CENTRAL	10.7656	3.6068	4
MOUNTAIN	6.2857	3.6745	8
PACIFIC	6.6477	3.6075	5

virtually all economic indicators of poverty classify American Indians as the "poorest of the poor" in our country, why are their homicide rates so much lower than those of the Black population? One answer may be that the Indian population also has high rates of aggression directed inward in the form of suicide, which provides an alternative outlet for aggression. Frustration is, therefore, vented in several different forms so that no one specific type may be especially high. Two theories may be useful analytic tools for understanding this possible spillover effect: the culture of self-directed violence and the culture of other-directed violence theories. These two complementary theories emphasize the cultural factors that can both inhibit and disinhibit certain groups from engaging in aggressive acts.

The term *culture of other-directed violence* is often used to describe research that focuses on violence directed outward against another. Homicide would be an example of other-directed violence. Wolfgang and Ferracuti's (1967) research on the subculture of violence provides one of the most comprehensive theoretical examinations of subcultures and homicide. Their work has provided the main theoretical base for much of the research in this area.

The subculture of violence thesis suggests that a lot of deviant behavior is a reflection of normative support for deviant values by a subgroup and even of encouragement by certain groups. This thesis further contends that violent behavior is a necessary and accepted way of life among certain groups and that these subcultures pass on attitudes and beliefs as to the accepted use of physical aggression in conflict situations. The choices in resolving a conflict situation are limited to culturally learned responses such as violence, especially when interacting with persons of a comparable culture. According to the subculture of violence argument, situations are most likely to trigger culturally accepted violence when an individual's character has been questioned, ridiculed, or insulted. The individual uses physical aggression to defend personal character, which sometimes leads to the death of one of the parties involved.

The ideas for defining a culture of self-directed violence are drawn from the research of Palmer and Humphrey (1978; also see Palmer, 1972). These authors hypothesize that attitudes and values in certain subcultures of the population encourage behavior that is harmful to the self, such as alcohol abuse and suicide. They further believe that both self- and other-directed subcultures can flourish within the same population:

The suggestion here is that subcultures of self-directed violence contain customs and values which advocate various forms of self-destructive behavior which vary in quality and degree: over smoking, alcoholism, drug abuse, and other behaviors harmful to physical and psychological health, with suicide simply the most extreme form. (p. 109)

If we analyze American Indian, White, and Black rates of both homicide and suicide, the proposition that some cultural element may be dictating aggressive outlets seems highly plausible. Homicide and suicide can be described as acts that are at opposite ends on a continuum of aggression, with homicide representing the most extreme form of aggression directed outward toward another individual, and suicide representing the most extreme form of aggression directed inward.

Figures 2.6 and 2.7 present homicide and suicide rates for American Indians, Blacks, and Whites for the years 1965-1983. The data used for the numerator in suicide rate calculations were obtained from the Vital Statistics of the United States. Homicide rates reported in Figure 2.6 reflect offender arrest rates from the Uniform Crime Reports. All denominators were obtained from the U.S. Census for the years 1960, 1970, and 1980. A linear procedure was used to estimate the population growth between the Census years. These numbers were then used as the denominators to calculate rates that fell between Census counts.

If we use homicide as an indicator of other-directed violence and suicide to represent the acts of self-directed violence, some rather interesting trends emerge. From Figure 2.6 it can be seen that Blacks have consistently had the highest homicide rates in our nation, while Whites have had the lowest. American Indian homicide rates, although lower than

Figure 2.6
Homicide Offender Rates by Ethnicity, 1965-1983

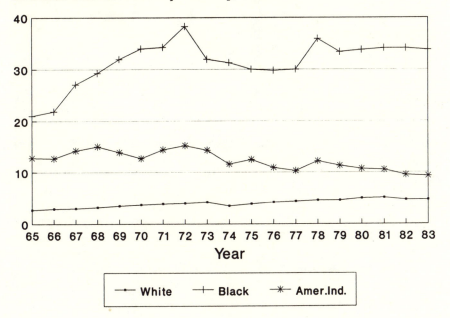

those of the black population, have been twice as high as those of the White population for the entire time period.

Figure 2.7 displays the suicide death rates by race/ethnicity. The picture that can be seen from this figure is quite different from that of Figure 2.6. American Indian suicide rates are the highest on average for the period 1968 to 1977 when compared with either the White or the Black population, with Whites barely surpassing them in the latter part of the time period. The Black population has consistently had the lowest annual suicide rate of the three racial/ethnic groups.

The juxtapositional image that emerges from Figures 2.6 and 2.7 is very interesting. It appears that the Black population has the highest rate of turning aggression outward in the form of homicide. In contrast, Whites more often turn their aggression inward in the form of suicide. American Indians, on the other hand, have high rates of *both* internal and external aggression. This pattern is consistent for all years analyzed.

To illuminate race/ethnicity differences for the two extreme forms of internal and external aggression, a suicide/homicide ratio measure was computed [suicide rate/(suicide rate + homicide rate)]. This ratio allows quantificaiton of a population's propensity to commit suicide over homicide. For example, the larger the ratio, the greater the incidence of suicide for a population category, whereas a small ratio score indicates a

Figure 2.7
Suicide Rates by Ethnicity, 1965-1983

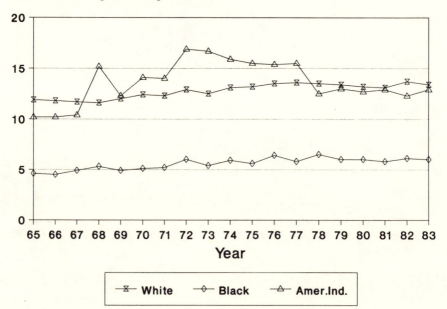

greater incidence of homicide. A ratio score of .5 indicates no difference in the propensity to commit either homicide or suicide. Table 2.4 displays the suicide-homicide ratios for each racial/ethnic group. From this table it is clear that, in every comparison year, Whites were more likely to direct their frustrations inward in the form of suicide compared to homicide. Conversely, Blacks, who had the lowest ratio scores, were consistently more likely to commit homicide than suicide. American Indian ratio scores hovered around the .5 level. This indicates that the American Indian population appears to have a nondiscriminating tolerance for both internal and external acts of violence.

Interpreting these ratios from a subculture of violence perspective, it appears that Blacks may exist within a subculture where acts of outward aggression are more acceptable than are aggressive acts directed inward. The White population, however, more often inhibits acts of other-directed violence, yet tolerates self-directed violence. American Indians appear to live in a subcultural milieu in which both external and internal forms of violence are tolerated.

The question now becomes, Why does there exist this apparent cultural difference in targets of violence? Why is the self sometimes chosen over

Table 2.4
Suicide/Homicide Ratio Scores by Race/Ethnicity, 1965-1983

Year	White	Black	American Indian
		SUICIDE/HOMICIDE RATIO SCORE*	
1965	.81	.17	.44
1966	.80	.17	.44
1967	.79	.15	.42
1968	.78	.15	.50
1969	.77	.13	.46
1970	.77	.13	.52
1971	.75	.13	.49
1972	.76	.13	.52
1973	.74	.14	.53
1974	.78	.15	.57
1975	.77	.15	.55
1976	.76	.17	.58
1977	.75	.16	.60
1978	.74	.15	.50
1979	.74	.15	.53
1980	.72	.15	.54
1981	.71	.14	.55
1982	.74	.15	.56
1983	.74	.15	.58

*Suicide/Homicide Ratio Score = [Suicide Rate/(Suicide Rate + Homicide Rate)]

others as a legitimate target for aggression? As early as 1958, Gold postulated that the mode or modes of aggression selected depend to a great extent on the culture in which the individual participates. The vast differences in the social, economic, and political histories of these racial/ethnic groups are partially responsible for the separate cultures that have developed for each of these groups. The White population has, on the whole, had the advantage of both political and economic power in this country. Culturally, political institutions and economic power provide outlets for risk taking and aggression, and success is measured by the ability to perform well in these fields of endeavor. Failure is blamed on the individual. This type of cultural background better enables the individual to blame the self for all types of problems and failures. This may, in turn, lead to higher rates of self-directed behavior like suicide. It has also been argued that the unique history of Black Americans (i.e., slavery, economic powerlessness, and so on) has contributed to a subculture in which life is devalued and other-directed violence is viewed as an important defense of masculinity (Wolfgang & Ferracuti, 1967; Hackney, 1969; Gastil, 1971).

What is of interest for purposes of this book is the fact that the American Indian population seems to have elements of both self- and other-directed violent subcultures coexisting within its cultural environment. This population's position of economic and political powerlessness within American society must certainly contribute to the development of such a subculture. The American Indian population may live in such a state of frustration and blocked opportunities that both inward and outward forms of aggression are readily utilized and tolerated. The sanctity of all life, one's own and others', is devalued. As Chapter 1 documented, poverty and unemployment are often a way of life for many American Indians. When a population is relegated to a colonized status and given little economic or political power, it is not difficult to envision the "fatalistic" environment in which those within that population must exist. Within an atmosphere such as this, violence appears to take both inward and outward directions, resulting in high rates of homicide and suicide.

The utilization of this cultural explanation here is in no way meant to diminish the importance of structural explanations such as economic deprivation. I have focused attention on subcultural explanations, however, to aid in our understanding of how national rates of American Indian homicide may be diminished, in comparison to those of other groups, because alternative outlets for aggression exist within this population. The analysis of both homicide and suicide rates suggests that American Indians may have developed a subculture of *both* self- and other-directed violence. By providing two cultural channels for aggression resulting from blocked opportunities, this cultural agent may be responsible for keeping American Indian homicide rates lower than rates in the Black population. However, it is important to note again that these national rates sometimes mask extremely high rates of homicide in certain reservation communities, as we will see in Chapter 4.

While this chapter has documented that American Indians are at a greater risk of homicide than is the White population, it does not tell us why. Although the commonality in homicide patterns among the different groups examined in this chapter may suggest that the fundamental causes of homicide may be much the same regardless of race or ethnicity, the etiology of American Indian homicide begs closer examination. Chapter 3 will outline a theoretical model of American Indian homicide, which evolved from interviews with American Indian homicide offenders. This model incorporates many causal elements, both cultural and structural, which all contribute to increase the probability of homicide within the American Indian population.

The Social Causes of American Indian Homicide as Revealed by the Life Experiences of Offenders

As the previous chapter has documented, American Indians have one of the highest national homicide rates of all racial/ethnic groups in this country. Further, in Chapter 4 we will see that homicide rates sometimes reach monumental proportions when reservation county rates are examined. For example, some counties have American Indian homicide rates over 100 per 100,000 population (e.g., Douglas, Nev., 103.5; Harney, Or., 127.55). Other investigators have noted high rates of American Indian homicide as well.[1]

Descriptive analyses such as these have played an important role in documenting the seriousness of the problem. However, there have been virtually no attempts to explore the etiology of American Indian homicide. Are the causal mechanisms that create these homicide differentials the same as those that have been documented in the population in general? Or are the social forces that have been identified as increasing both Black and White homicide rates different from those forces that contribute to American Indian homicide?

The empirical results of the comparative homicide literature, which has investigated regional variations in homicide and also variations between Black and White homicide differentials, have remained equivocal. Some researchers advocate subcultural explanations of homicide rates,[2] while others contend that structural explanations such as economic deprivation, are better predictors of homicide.[3] Some of the inconsistency in this literature lies in methodological problems, such as the identification of a clear indicator of subcultural orientations, and other problems, such as correct model estimation.

These problems exist alongside the relative paucity of research that investigates homicide among American Indians. Because research that explores the etiology of American Indian homicide is virtually nonexistent in the literature, it would be a mistake to extract indicators from the existing literature and use them as a template for this study. It is first important to gain insight and understanding of the structural and cultural conditions that may contribute to lethal violence in this racial/ethnic group.

This chapter presents an analysis of interviews that were conducted with a sample of thirty incarcerated American Indians who were convicted of homicide. By qualitatively examining these offenders' unique background characteristics, their attitudes about the crime they committed and about crime in general, and the circumstances that surrounded their crimes, concepts emerge that allow us to outline a theoretical guide for American Indian homicide. This guide contains elements of social disorganization, economic deprivation, a subculture of violence, and culture conflict and perceived powerlessness, as well as an intervening variable of alcohol/drug abuse. Also included in the model is the antecedent variable of internal colonialism. By identifying these sensitizing concepts, the quantitative analysis presented in Chapter 4 is more responsibly informed.

METHODS

Face-to-face, in-depth interviews were conducted with thirty homicide offenders from July 1988 to January 1989 at three midwestern state prisons. All interviews were conducted by this author. These sites were selected because they had a comparatively large number of American Indian homicide offenders and allowed the interviews to be performed. Sample selection was obviously not random and thus may not be representative of all American Indian homicide offenders.

The average age of the offenders was twenty-eight, with an age range of twenty to fifty-three years. Only two had graduated from high school; however, all but one had passed the General Educational Development Test while in prison. Most were unemployed at the time of the homicide, and those who were not were underemployed. Five of the offenders were married, four were divorced, and twenty-one were single.

Characteristics of these offenders' homicides are displayed in Table 3.1. For comparison purposes, Table 3.1 also provides the corresponding national homicide percentages for American Indians, Blacks, and Whites that were highlighted in Chapter 2. It is important to note that the characteristics of this sample's homicides are very similar to those observed at the national level for the American Indian population.

The majority of homicide victims in this sample were acquaintances of the offenders, and most of the homicides were committed during a conflict situation or argument. The most frequent weapon used was a knife, followed by a gun. One of the most striking facts to emerge from Table

Table 3.1
Sample Characteristics of the Offenders' Crimes and Criminal Records (*N* = 30) and Comparable American Indian, White, and Black National Homicide Percentages, 1980-1984

	Sample Characteristics	American Indian Nat. Percent	White Nat. Percent	Black Nat. Percent
VICTIM/OFFENDER RELATIONSHIP				
Family	20% (6)	23%	26%	21%
Acquaintance	53%(16)	60%	46%	58%
Stranger	27% (8)	17%	28%	21%
CIRCUMSTANCE OF HOMICIDE				
Robbery	16% (5)	8%	10%	6%
Other Felony	10% (3)	3%	4%	2%
Conflict	67%(20)	51%	42%	52%
Gang Related	7% (2)	18%	19%	16%
WEAPON USED				
Knife	40%(12)	29%	20%	23%
Gun	33%(10)	46%	57%	64%
Beating or Blunt Obj.	20% (6)	15%	14%	9%
Threw From Balcony	3% (1)	NC	NC	NC
Ran Over With Car	3% (1)	NC	NC	NC
ALCOHOL/DRUG INFLUENCE DURING CRIME				
Under Influence of Alcohol/Drugs	97%(29)	NC	NC	NC
Under No Influence of Alcohol/Drugs	3% (1)	NC	NC	NC
PRIOR RECORD (JUVENILE OR OTHERWISE)				
Prior Record	93%(28)	NC	NC	NC
No Prior Record	7% (2)	NC	NC	NC

Note: The American Indian, White, and Black national percentage comparisons represent national rates that were converted to percentages. These percentages are for the years 1980-1984 and were obtained from the Supplementary Homicide Report collected by the Federal Bureau of Investigation as a part of its Uniform Crime Reporting program. The entire data set was compiled at the University of New Hampshire and is referred to as the Comparative Homicide File (CHF) (Williams and Flewelling, 1987); NC = No comparable figure at this national level.

3.1 is the involvement of these offenders with alcohol or drugs during the commission of the homicide. Ninety-seven percent of the offenders were under the influence of alcohol or drugs at the time of the homicide, and 93 percent had prior records (juvenile or otherwise).

THE INTERVIEW PROCESS

After answering several structured questions regarding demographics, such as age and place of birth, the offenders responded to a lengthy set of open-ended questions and probes concerning the circumstances sur-rounding their crime, their life before the crime, and their attitudes about crime in general. (The interview questionnaire is reproduced in Appendix A.) These questions were constructed to elicit data on their per-ceptions of the events that transpired and the possible contributors to the crime. Their beliefs and attitudes toward crime were of particular interest because these beliefs can illustrate subcultural orientations.

With the consent of the respondent, a tape recorder was used to ensure that complete and accurate data were obtained. All but one respondent agreed. Interviews lasted from two to three hours, with an average of approximately two hours. The process resembled a conversation between two people getting to know one another rather than a rigid structure in which questions were formally addressed. An interview was usually ended not because there was nothing left to talk about, but because another interview was scheduled or because the prisoner had to return to his cell for count.

THE LIVES OF AMERICAN INDIAN OFFENDERS

Although each of the thirty American Indian homicide offenders had a different life story to tell, their narratives share astounding similarities. Before breaking down their histories into fragmented pieces, however, I think it is important to examine a few case histories. This will provide the reader with a glimpse into the lives of these men, as well as insight into the reality that many American Indian youth in general must live with. To protect the anonymity of these men, I will simply refer to them by the order in which they were interviewed.

Respondent Eight

Respondent eight was born on a midwestern reservation—welcomed to the world by two alcoholic parents and four siblings. His earliest memories are of hiding in the bedroom with his brothers and sisters during his parents' frequent drunken fights with each other. His father was sporadically employed, and his mother stayed home caring for the children. Stable moments were few and far between. When asked about happy memories, he replies, "Yeah, when my parents were sober I guess I was happy. I loved them very much but when they were drunk, which was most every weekend, I was scared—especially of my father. If we ever tried to stop him from hurting my mother or one of us—we would get it."

By age eleven, he was sniffing glue and drinking whenever he and his friends could get their hands on alcohol. School was going relatively well up to this point, but cutting class soon became the rule rather than the exception. His parents had divorced, and he now lived with his mother and a new stepfather. The violence at home was diminished, but not gone, and the drunkenness continued.

At age fifteen, he stole his first car. "We were just tired of the res and wanted to go to the city." This joy ride sent him to a juvenile detention center. Here his identity as an Indian was solidified; there was a definite segregation between the White and the Indian youths. "On the res you know there was white people but we just tended to stay away from them—or I guess they stayed away from us. When they did talk to us it was basically giving us shit about who we were—you know like 'scum sucking Indians' and stuff like that." Now a member of an Indian group at the detention center, his hatred toward White people intensified, as did his hatred for the world in general.

After his release, he returned to the reservation. His drinking increased in both intensity and frequency, and he was soon experimenting with other drugs. He found a job as a gas station attendant, but lost it because of alcohol. Four months after his release from the detention center, he left the reservation to return to the city, and a month later he was arrested on a burglary charge. He recalls, "The cops would beat me but I would just keep getting up. That was one thing I would never do no matter how much it hurt. I would never stay down." He describes this to me as he points out the scar that runs from his forehead across his eye to his cheek. "They almost put an eye out," he adds.

Following his second release, he remained in the city. He could not find work and so spent his days drinking and living with friends and distant relatives.

Six months later, he and an accomplice stabbed to death an unsuspecting homeowner while they were burglarizing his home. They had been drinking, and although they had no intention of murder that night, he recalls:

He came in and surprised us. I just remember feeling a tremendous amount of anger—I just kept stabbing and stabbing, not really even thinking of that man but just thinking about everything—the system, the injustice—everything. I thought to myself that I would get caught for sure but I wasn't going down without a fight.

I remember running downtown and I had gotten a gun. I figured if they tried to get me I would shoot and try to get as many of those bastards as I could before they killed me.

Respondent eight was apprehended and disarmed before any shooting could take place. He was later convicted of first-degree murder. "You know when I'm talking on this tape I don't know why you want to hear my story. It's all trouble. All bad. All courts and doing time. Why would anyone want to know about this?"

Respondent Fifteen

Respondent fifteen was born in the city and only made infrequent trips to the reservation to visit relatives. Most of his youth was spent living in the projects of the inner city with his mother and younger brother. His father who had left the family when the respondent was four years old, only visited when "he wanted money or booze."

While he does not remember many "good times" during his childhood, he has some fond memories of grade school. "I spent most of my time reading back then—escaping into books. I read about Indians and about cars. They never taught us anything about Indians in school so I had to read on my own."

By junior high school, however, things were much different. His Indian identity was now a hindrance to his acceptance by peers. "They just gave me shit all the time. Calling me names and picking fights." He found his niche with another American Indian friend in a street gang. By the age of fourteen, he was successfully socialized into gang life. Not only was he adept at using most drugs, but he also knew how to make money selling them. "I was successful by the time I was 16. I had my own car and my own apartment. I had goals and I knew how to get what I wanted." For respondent fifteen, the means for achieving material success was not through a nine-to-five job, but rather through selling drugs and stealing. Gang life had not only taught him these trades, but also instilled in him the importance of standing up for oneself and one's territory.

Although he will point out the battle scars he sustained during gang fights, he will more eagerly tell you of those he skillfully inflicted on others. One act of revenge on a member of another gang took place when he cut the brake wires in a rival gang member's car. "He had this real nice classic old car. I wanted to get him and the car. The only bad thing was that his little brother was in the car with him when it hit a pole doing about 45 [mph]. I felt bad about the kid." Neither of the boys were killed, but they were "racked up pretty bad for awhile—broken legs and shit."

He talks of another time when he was sent to the hospital for numerous stab wounds sustained during a street fight.

It's one of the only times I remember really feeling cared about. My friends all came to see me every day. They walked with me down the hall for exercise with all the IV tubes. They even brought me shit—even two girls stole some shit for me—good shit. They said, "We got you a drum set" 'cause they knew I liked to play, and I thought it would be some piece of junk, but it was a real nice Ludwig set. I couldn't believe it. I mean they really cared. I haven't felt that good in a long time.

Respondent fifteen was placed in juvenile hall twice on various drug and theft charges. His next conviction was for first-degree murder. He was sentenced to life in prison after being convicted of beating an elderly woman to death during a burglary.

Respondent Twenty-Two

Respondent twenty-two was also the child of alcoholic parents, but was put in a White foster home at the age of three. He and his sister were separated from their older brother, who was placed in a different foster home. When respondent twenty-two was in the third grade, they were all moved into the same foster home. This was his fourth move and third foster home.

By seventh grade, he was running away from home. "I started hanging around people who were older than me." By eighth grade he was doing drugs and drinking and had stabbed another boy in a fight. Defending himself and his honor was important to him. By age fourteen he ran away back to the reservation. He lived with whomever he could for awhile, but soon ended up in another foster home and had now been separated from his biological siblings for over one year. He was placed in a public school off the reservation with mostly "white kids." By age sixteen he was back in the "work house" for car theft and after release was back in again for theft.

Soon after his eighteenth birthday, he was partying with some friends. "Some guy who was bigger than me—about 6'2"—kept bugging me. He wouldn't leave me alone. So I had this knife—it was just for show but things just got out of hand. He kept pushing me and pushing me. I had to stand up for myself—just because he was bigger than me—I'm not scared of nobody." Respondent twenty-two was convicted of second-degree murder for the stabbing death of another young Indian male while under the influence of alcohol.

A THEORETICAL GUIDE FOR AMERICAN INDIAN HOMICIDE

Figure 3.1 displays the guide for American Indian homicide that evolved from the analysis of homicide offender interviews. The guide combines

Figure 3.1
Theoretical Model for American Indian Homicide

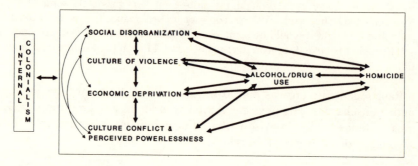

the causal forces of social disorganization, economic deprivation, a culture of violence, and the psychological mechanisms of culture conflict and perceived powerlessness with the intervening variable of alcohol/drug abuse. Also included in the guide is the antecedent variable to each of these concepts of internal colonialism. While this was not explicitly derived from the qualitative analysis, no model explaining any phenomenon with regard to American Indians would be complete without acknowledgment of the colonization process to which our government has subjected this population.

The remainder of this chapter will review previous theoretical work on which the concepts of this model were predicated and then illustrate each concept with interview narratives.

Internal Colonialism

> When you look back in history you see many things. You know religion manipulates people. For example, did you know that over 90 percent of South America is Catholic? And most of those people are Indians—the creator gave them something different but that organized, manipulative religion stepped in. You know I've read books. There are the Cambodians—millions of them killed and people had their eyes shut just like they did when the Jews had their Holocaust and the Russians—everyone looks at all these tragedies but nobody looks right here at the tragedy in North America. There is a holocaust right here. When the white man came, there were over 200 million Indians in both Canada and here. Now there are only about 5 million. Wouldn't you call that a holocaust? Not only death of a people but death of our culture. They have nothing now—not heritage, not identity—nothing. And when you have nothing you turn to something else—drugs, alcohol, violence. That's why there is all this unemployment, suicide, drug and alcohol abuse, all this death and killing. We don't have a culture. We don't have nothing. (Respondent twenty-two)

This quote vividly depicts the possible effects of internal colonialism as perceived by one homicide offender. The concept of internal colonialism stems from the writings of Blauner (1972), who describes four components of the colonization complex:

Colonization begins with a forced, involuntary entry. Second there is an impact on the culture and social organization of the colonized people which is more than just a result of such "natural" processes as contact and acculturation. The colonizing power carries out a policy which constrains, transforms, or destroys indigenous values, orientations, and ways of life. Third, colonization involves a relationship by which members of the colonized group tend to be administered by representatives of the dominant power. There is an experience of being managed and manipulated by outsiders in terms of ethnic status. A final fundament of colonization is racism. Racism is a principle of social domination by which a group seen as inferior or different in terms of alleged biological characteristics is exploited, controlled, and oppressed socially and psychically by a superordinate group. (Blauner, 1969, p. 396)

The European conquest of American Indian populations typifies the process of internal colonialism. From the first European contact with the original population in the New World to the present day, American Indians have been relegated to a colonized status. History tells a story of brutalization, exploitation, segregation, expulsion, and, for some tribes, annihilation.

In the mid-nineteenth century, the U.S. government embarked on a policy of containment as a means of controlling the Indians and encouraging westward expansion. Military force was used to displace many tribes and resettle them on wasteland reservations, where they remained unless new settlement plans or the discovery of oil and valuable minerals resulted in further displacement. Virtually all of the original tribal nations were separated or absorbed into other groups, if not exterminated altogether. The cultural heritage of many was forever altered, if not completely obliterated. This colonization process continues today. Almost every facet of Indian life is controlled by our government, including important elements of the culture such as religion. The recent U.S. Supreme Court decision allowing restrictions on peyote use in religious ceremonies is but one example.[4] The case, *Employment Division v. Smith*, involved two Oregon men, both members of the Native American Church, who were fired from their jobs and denied unemployment benefits for participating in a sacramental rite that involves ingesting peyote. The Supreme Court ruled that legislatures can exempt religious conduct from certain laws (i.e., drug laws), but that there is no constitutional requirement that they do so. This decision was devastating for those who engage in less widely used religious practices such as peyote use. It was, perhaps, no coincidence that those who primarily engage in the religious practice of peyote use were relatively powerless, both economically and politically: American Indians. This is, unfortunately, just one example of political acts that perpetuate the colonization process today.

An in-depth historical review of Native American/White relations is not the purpose here; other writers have provided important accounts of these already.[5] My purpose is to acknowledge the process of containment and exploitation that most American Indian people in this country have experienced. This process is perhaps the earliest antecedent to some of the present deleterious conditions under which many American Indians live, including the other contributors of homicide outlined in Figure 3.1. This colonization process has undoubtedly contributed to economic deprivation and social disorganization within American Indian populations.

Social Disorganization

> I was pretty much living in foster homes since I was about two. I guess my parents weren't doing too good—you know, drinking and partying. My brother got put into a different foster home, but my sister and I got in the same one. After several moves, we all eventually got placed in the same home. We moved around quite a bit. (Respondent three)

The foundation for the social disorganization perspective stems from one of Durkheim's arguments that rapid social change is associated with increases in crime due to a breakdown of social controls. It emerged in the writings and research of sociologists at the University of Chicago during the 1920s. The initial formulator was Thomas, with other contributors following, including Park and Burgess (1921), and Shaw and McKay (1969). Probably the most concise statement of this perspective is found in the classic study conducted by Thomas and Znaniecki (1920). According to these authors, social disorganization was to be defined as a decrease in the influence of existing social rules of behavior on individual members of the group. When a society is in a state of social disorganization, people are set free of normative constraints, leading increasing numbers of people to drift from conformity into deviance.

Virtually all of the homicide offenders interviewed share similar life histories, and most of these histories contain indicators of social disorganization. Approximately 40 percent of those interviewed spent part of their lives in foster homes, 6 percent were adopted, and another 13 percent were sent to boarding schools at a young age. Of those in foster homes, virtually all were sent to at least two different homes during their life. Further, not only were many separated from their biological parents, but also, of those sent to foster homes or adopted, many were separated from their siblings at one time or another. It is not the purpose of this research to explore the reasons for the separation of these people from their families. However, some authors believe that such separations are without just cause or due process. It has been documented that Indian children are removed from their families much more frequently than are children in non-Indian populations.[6]

This family disruption is very likely to have contributed to an environment of social disorganization in the lives of these homicide offenders. As the family is usually the center of an individual's emotional life, assaults on Indian families through separation contribute to feelings of hopelessness and powerlessness. In addition to experiencing the trauma of separation from their families, the men I interviewed had to cope with the problems of adjusting to a social and cultural enviornment much different from their own. One offender told of his first encounter with the White couple who had adopted him:

> The social worker took me and my brother to a hotel room where we stayed overnight. I remember my brother just crying all night. I was nine and he was just six. I mean we didn't even know why we were taken from our parents. They just did it. Then the next day this young white couple came to the room—they couldn't have been older than 25 at the time. We only had a couple of suitcases but my Dad had given me a box of stuff he wanted me to have. He had given me special stuff and two of his guns. The first thing the white guy said was, "What's in the box?" He opened it up and saw the guns and broke them right away and then said, "We don't allow guns in our house." Right away I knew I was in for trouble. I mean he didn't even think about my feelings. They were my Dad's and he had given them to me. That's the way it was until I started running away when I was about 13.

Even more poignant was the personal narrative of an older prisoner who told of being taken from his family to attend a boarding school. "I was just holding on to my mother's dress and screaming. My mother was crying, too. They literally dragged me away and put me on a bus with other crying kids."

While the youths sent to boarding schools may have had group support for their identities, the youths placed in foster and adoptive homes had to integrate themselves into different racial and cultural milieus as well as attempt to solve their personal identity problems. It is not the intent here to condemn the good intentions of the foster and adoptive parents in these cases. Some offenders felt deep love for the families who had taken them in. One states, "They're the only ones who I really want to think good of me. I owe it to them to try to straighten things out."

But beyond the benevolence of these families, how could the cultural transmission of Indian heritage be performed properly? Respondent ten stated, "They took me to a pow wow once or twice. That's what they thought being Indian was."

Park (1967) states, "The process by which the authority and influence of an earlier culture and system of social control is undermined and eventually destroyed is . . . social disorganization." This disorganization was clearly evident in the lives of the homicide offenders interviewed. Those who were separated from their families were quickly thrust into a foreign environment, leaving behind all previous normative guidelines. This may have left many in a state of normlessness and may have propelled some of them into juvenile delinquency and ultimately murder.

Disorganization was present in another form as well. Although other inmates were not separated from their families, the presence of alcoholic parents often produced instability in their lives. The family unit for these offenders was not characterized by secure routine, but rather was complicated by frequent and sporadic drinking binges on the part of one or both parents. This often meant being left alone for an evening, and sometimes days, without adult supervision. As respondent seventeen states:

> I lived with my Mom mostly but moved back and forth between my Mom and my Dad's a lot. My Mom lived on the reservation and my Dad lived different places at different times. My environment was always changing. I'd go from my Mom who liked to party on Friday nights or Saturday nights; she would sometimes go two or three weeks without partying but then start drinking again. Then I would go to my Dad who liked to party everyday—if there were eight days in a week, he would party eight days. So I went from a mellow environment to an extreme. It was hard for me to adjust.

This condition was undoubtedly a contributor to the social disorganization experienced by these children and, further, could have served to sabotage normative guidance.

Of course, many American Indians who are similarly children of alcoholics or who are placed in foster/adoptive homes may become well-adjusted adults. The offenders in this study, however, had more difficulty avoiding the negative behavioral and psychological consequences that social disorganization can produce. Further, the disorganization present in the lives of these men seems to have fostered and intensified the culture conflict that may or may not have already existed.

Culture Conflict

> Many Indians today find themselves in a psychological no-man's land as a result of the impact of the dominant culture on Indian values. Most young Indian people now share similar educational

experiences with the typical teenager of today. They no longer wear the tribal costume, and they speak the common languge. They, also, are victims of television and followers of the latest fad. They have all the problems common to the youth of the country, and in addition, the special problem of making satisfactory psychological reconcilia-tions with the mores of two cultures.[7]

The above quote graphically depicts the psychological state of many young American Indians, who may be experiencing culture conflict between the dominant White culture and their own Indian identity. Many other authors have noted this concept as well.[8] Berlin (1987) states that "pressures to make it in Anglo ways because very few are making it in the old ways result in serious conflict between contradictory values" (p. 224). Others have documented that this culture conflict is often a precursor of violent behavior. For example, Frederick (1973) believes that every young Indian must ask himself or herself this question: "shall I live in the white man's world or in the world of the Indian?" He further notes that the two life styles do not always merge, helping lacunae and conflicts to appear "Young Indians grow up without a satisfactory identifi-cation either with their own heritage or with that of white society" (p. 8).

Culture conflict was experienced by virtually all of the offenders inter-viewed. Although the extent to which it may have played a role in the homicides cannot be determined, it must be included in any causal model of this phenomenon. One respondent's powerful description should help the reader to understand, as much as can be understood, what culture conflict is to some American Indians:

I was reading this religious book and it asked, "Are you in the valley of conflicting beliefs?" I hadn't really thought about it before but when I did, I thought boy, I sure am. You know you have the Catho-lics and the Lutherans and all these people saying this is the way—the Jews are over there and the Muslims. Everyone trying to pull your arm. That's the way my whole life was. When I was little on the reservation, they wouldn't let us practice our traditional reli-gion—they sent all us little kids to Catholic school. Then when I was adopted and moved off the reservation, they pushed Presbyterian on me. You know when I look at the reservations—they are full of Cath-olic churches—you know it's just trying to take all of the Indian culture away from the people—trying to assimilate them. It's not being passed down anymore. Even my grandparents and parents were beaten when they spoke their language. That's two generations of culture lost and I'm the third. I'm just finding myself and my culture now in here. It was inside of me all the time and it feels good. It feels right. If I was born in the Middle East or something, I would have something else inside me, but this was meant to be. It's too bad I had to find it in prison. I'm the one that was robbed.

Another reveals how this conflict manifested itself at an early age:

> What I remember most about growing up was being poor, but the other thing that stands out most is being Indian in a mostly white school. I knew I was Indian—I would draw Indian pictures and stuff and read Indian stories. But to me if I tried to be one to everyone else, I would just get teased so I only did that stuff when nobody was around. I wanted to fit in, but it never happened. I would get in a lot of fights and shit. By third grade I was in a gang—all the misfits, I guess—we formed this gang and we were mean.

This is illustrative of how this conflict can sometimes contribute to violence. Respondent two shed light on one of the intricacies of the conflict. It is not only a matter of fitting into one or the other culture; it is also often experienced along with an element of discrimination.

> Right now there are Indian kids on the street just like I used to be—smoking pot and drinking. They don't know where to fit in. There is not really an Indian culture anymore and the whites don't accept them. This government has tried forcing us to adopt the white ways, but we need to find our heritage—ourselves. I know we can't go back to hunting buffalo, but we can't do anything unless we have an identity.

Another offender describes this culture conflict and how it was intensified by being placed in a White foster home:

> Like growing up in a white family when you're an Indian is a little strange. They really wanted me to be like them and I wanted to. I loved them. They did take me to a few pow wows when I was just a little guy so I knew I was an Indian, but I didn't really know what an Indian was. The only thing I knew was that I was an Indian but that Indians weren't that good. Even in school you only heard about the bad stuff and all the TV shows were showing Indians as savages and shit. Even now on the news and stuff where are the Indians represented? When I watch TV in here and when they give a poll or something, you hear what the whites, the blacks, even the orientals have to say. They get their opinions heard, but not us. The only things you hear are bad—like "Oh! That Indian suicide and that Indian drinking—they have problems." What about the good in my people?

Another offender describes an experience he had in the service during the Vietnam War:

> I had an incident happen when I went into the service—it was right after Martin Luther King got shot. I was sent to basic training down

south on a bus and at the first stop for the bathrooms—the bathrooms were labeled colored and white. I didn't know which one to go in so I didn't. I waited until I got back to the fort. It was a long ride back.

This recollection was humorous, and he laughed as he told me about it. However, his face soon went somber, and he said, "I can laugh about it now."

Many of the offenders I talked with had found a part of their cultural identity within the prison walls. All prison sites provided and even encouraged participation in Indian religious ceremonies (i.e., pipe carrying and sweat lodges). A psychologist at one of the prison sites described the stabilizing reaction he noticed in American Indian offenders after they had participated in these activities. "They will often come in very uptight and withdrawn. But once they get involved in the Indian group and the Indian culture, you can just see the change. It is like they have finally found a part of themselves. Most have never had the opportunity to do these things until prison." Respondent four gives validity to this observation:

I've seen what happens when people find themselves—find their identity and their heritage. You can take a drunken Indian and give him culture and self-esteem and watch him change for the better. I've known people who were on the wrong road—even a few who were in jail before—but some of the programs they got going now are teaching them the culture—the language and the religion. Now I know a few who even have their master's degrees now, and they are coming back and helping their people. You see you can't get nothing together without getting your own stuff together.

The negative consequences that this culture conflict may have for psychological adjustment are great. It is hard for members of the dominant society to empathize with the feelings of powerlessness and insecurity that minority group members experience during the process of "finding" themselves, even though we all share similar agonies. But for those of us who have the privilege of having white skin in a predominantly White society, it is hard to grasp the possible magnitude and intensity of these feelings. This is particularly true when an American Indian is struggling with both the usual identity problems of youth and the identity problems of being Indian in a White society—an identity that is too often confronted with negative stereotypes and discrimination in our society. Moreover, when this culture conflict is played out in an environment that is already riddled with such maladies as unemployment, poverty, and social disorganization, the effects may sometimes be manifested in acts of lethal violence.

Although this phenomenon could only have been uncovered at the individual level, other possible cultural and structural contributors of American Indian homicide were also illuminated in these interviews. Discussions of both the subculture of violence and economic depriva- tion, which existed in the lives of these homicide offenders, follow.

Subculture of Violence

> When I was younger, I had to go out and pick fights, but by the time I was 15 I had a reputation and people came to pick fights with me. You know, challenging me and stuff. A lot of people would quit because they would think of things they had to lose, but me, I had my reputation—I had my pride. Even in fights where it could have been life or death, that's all I fought for—pride. (Respondent twenty)

Wolfgang (1958) believed that a culture of violence tolerates and even encourages physical force in conflict situations. "Quick resort to physical combat as a measure of daring, courage, or defense of status appears to be a cultural expression" (p. 188). The opening quotation from one of the homicide offenders I interviewed illustrates Wolfgang's theory, which is usually referred to as the subculture of violence theory. This theory focuses on the role of ideas in causing criminal behaviors. Wolfgang and Ferracuti (1967) state:

What the subculture of violence formulation suggests is simply that there is a potent theme of violence current in the cluster of values that make up the life- style, the socialization process, and the interpersonal relationships of individuals living in similar conditions. (p. 140)

This formulation was primarily based on an earlier study of homicide in Philadelphia by Wolfgang (1958). From the results of this study, Wolf- gang and Ferracuti (1967) concluded that a large number of homicides seemed to result from very trivial events that took on great importance because of mutually held expectations about how people would behave. The authors state:

The significance of a jostle, a slightly derogatory remark, or the appearance of a weapon in the hands of an adversary are stimuli differentially perceived and interpreted. . . . Social expectations of response in particular types of social inter- action result in differential definitions of the situation. A male is usually expected to defend the name or honor of his mother, the virtue of womanhood . . . and to accept no derogation about his race (even from a member of his own race), his age or his masculinity. When such a culture norm response is elicited from an individual engaged in social interplay with others who harbor the same response mechanism, physical assaults, altercations, and violent domestic quarrels that result in homicide are likely to be common. (pp. 188-89)

Extracting from the interview narratives, it appears that many of the respondents adhered to norms of "protecting your honor" first and foremost. For example, one offender explicitly described the learning process he went through as a child:

> It's important for me to be able to defend myself and fight. My dad taught me when I was really young how to fight. And when I have a son the first thing I will teach him is how to fight. How to stand up for himself. How to be brave. If you can't stand up for yourself and your honor you may as well not live anyway.

Many other narratives revealed the same cultural norms. One man stated, "People should have a right to defend themselves—themselves, their family, their house—everything. The law is funny. You should have that right." Another offender described beating other schoolchildren up when they called him names:

> When I was in school I would get in fights with white kids and I remember really trying to hurt them—not just fight but really try to kill them. It wasn't like fights with my brothers or friends. Especially when they cut me down—you know I had long hair and shit. They would tease me. I would go out of my way—not just punching them up but stomping their face and hitting their head on the sidewalk. This was when I was young—probably second or third grade. It was like "you go ahead and do that—do that to me—call me names and see what happens."

This quote illustrates the importance of defending one's honor within a cultural milieu that encourages or tolerates the use of physical force in such situations. Another respondent talked about an incident when he was close to death as the result of a knife fight. The foremost thought in his mind was that he had stood up and had defended himself, even though he was not armed:

> Anyone who messes with me better be prepared. One time, though, I got sliced up pretty bad and I was in the hospital. I was laying there, I had blood all over my chest and I was stabbed in the face. I remember thinking this is it. I remember the doctors and nurses saying "he's not responding" and everything—the priest was even there. I was like floating—not really there. But the last thing I do remember was thinking "I gave that son-of-a-bitch his—I showed him." Of course, not as good as he got me, but I did give him his. I still wish I knew he had a knife. I know how to defend myself. I've had a lot of experience with people coming at me with knives if I had only known.

Another offender used this analogy when describing the importance of defending oneself: "You know just like a dog will fight another dog if he enters his yard and the same dog will get it if he enters another dog's yard. It's fight to the death and that's the way it is. You protect yourself and your interests."

Although sentiments such as these were very visible within the dialogues of many offenders, it is not so clear exactly where they originated. Some talked of learning "the way to get respect" at an early age. Other statements seemed to demonstrate that these norms and values may have been internalized through institutional environments (i.e., in reform school or prison). For example, "There are groups here. The blacks, the Indians, the bikers. And some of these guys will go off at the slightest thing and you have to stand up to them or soon you'll be nothing but stepped on." Two other quotes reveal what living by the convict code means:

> Even in prison here, a lot of these guys are just soft. They don't live by the code. When you have a scrap with someone, you don't go running to the guards or caseworkers—you take care of it on your own. You know I've gotten into things with people who were a lot bigger. One black guy in here was giving me a hard time and I took him on—he even had a black belt in karate. I told him if he wanted to scrap with me—let's go! You get respect that way.

> Too many of the guys in here are just inmates—rapos and stuff— they're not convicts. There aren't many convicts left. You might think I'm young, but I've been in for a long time, and I know what the convict code is. You take care of your own problems—you don't go running for help or squealing.

Most of these offenders had been institutionalized on a number of occasions, and many at an early age. It is difficult to separate where one socialization process began and the other ended. Further, it is not clear how similar or dissonant these cultures may be. It is likely that both cultural sources, the Indian culture and the "convict culture," transmit norms and values that permit violent responses in conflict situations. It is clear, however, that a culture of violence does exist within this population, and although not accepted by everyone, it is acknowledged by most:

> I have a friend in here and he is smart, but he won't look at the things he does. If he would just apply his smarts positively—but I know he never will. He's too much into his image as a tough guy. Someone in the group will say "go beat this guy up" or "go burn his cell out" and he is right there doing it. All to keep that image up—it's like all he has. I used to do that shit too, but now I know it has taken more courage to sit in front of a group of white people and show my fears and insecurities than to go beat on somebody.

Again, it is not clear where the origins of these violent cultural norms lie. Numerous sources have contributed to instill them within certain segments of the American Indian population. The unique historical circumstances of the American Indian population almost certainly play a role—from the brutal extermination and relocation practices of the early Europeans against the Indian population to the near cultural genocide that resulted. Second, the early labeling and confinement processes of the juvenile justice system may also have contributed to these norms. A large proportion of these men were sent to work camps and juvenile detention centers at an early age. During this time, the rewards that were obtained for "masculine prowess" and bravery seem to have played an important role for some in their socialization process. This resulted in attitudes that were not only tolerant but also respectful of violence in response to certain situations. Violence in response to situations where one's honor or esteem is challenged was particularly revered by many of the offenders interviewed. And, finally, attitudes that support a culture of violence may have developed in response to the oppression and discrimination that many of these men experienced throughout their lives.

French and Hornbuckle (1977) have noted the similarities between the marginal Indians and the ghetto Blacks observed by Wolfgang and Ferracuti. They state:

Excluded from both the traditional subculture and the elite middle-class contingency present on the reservation, the marginal Indians are forced into a stress-ridden environment, one which allows for little social or personal autonomy. Instead they are torn between these two cultures following the respective dictates of each whenever possible. But for the most part, they must live in the chaotic world of their weak subculture—one based on retributive violence. Here violence is a common factor resulting from spontaneous eruption of frustrations.

In a world that has offered little economic and political power to the American Indian, overcompensating for this powerlessness in other aspects of their lives that can be controlled (i.e., personal relationships and confrontations) is a logical consequence.

Although Wolfgang and Ferracuti believe that subcultural ideas may have originated in general social conditions such as poverty, the cause of violent behavior was said to be the ideas themselves, rather than the conditions that had generated those ideas in the past. Past research seems to have created a false dichotomy between structural and cultural explanations of homicide. The model developed in this research posits that they are not causally separated, but act both alone *and* in combination to increase levels of lethal violence.

Economic Deprivation

You know when you don't have a job, you're just basically kicking back, hanging around. I remember just sitting around watching TV, and I'd get mad because I'd been to every damn employment agency. I'd gone and tried to get a job, and I remember coming back feeling frustrated, mad, just bored. To me, a man is supposed to provide, and when you're living off your aunt's check, that's just disgusting. I see it all the time. That's not the point. The point is you just feel useless—you got all that time. You see an ad in the paper, and you get all spiffed up and go down to apply and they say, "No, we can't use you." Pretty soon you just give them the finger and walk away. (Respondent two)

Economic deprivation can increase the likelihood of a number of pathologies, such as alcoholism, suicide, child abuse, and lethal violence. The psychological consequences of being poor are many. It engenders hopelessness, apathy, and anger. One form of coping with the alienation and hostility that poverty may produce is through aggression. The earliest theoretical work that links the economic structure of society with deviance comes from Merton (1968). In his theory of anomie, Merton defined *anomie* as a socially structured contradiction between the normative goals or aspirations of individuals in our society and the means available for legitimately attaining those goals. This contradiction between goals and means, Merton believed, had a direct relationship to deviant behavior. He believed that the probability of deviance increases when the "anybody can do it" aspirations of American society are confronted with the "not everybody has an equal chance" opportunity structure. Deviance was seen as a normal product of an unequal society.

Merton's theory was one of general deviance. With regard to the causation of homicide, Williams and Flewelling (1988) maintain that few investigators have really explained why such economic or resource deprivation should be positively associated with homicide rates. However, they claim that

it is reasonable to assume that when people live under conditions of extreme scarcity, the struggle for survival is intensified. Such conditions are often accompanied by a host of agitating psychological manifestations, ranging from a deep sense of powerlessness and brutalization to anger, anxiety, and alienation. Such manifestations can provoke physical aggression in conflict situations. (p. 423)

Although theoretical elaboration on economic sources of lethal violence is somewhat limited, empirical evidence is not.[9] As we discussed in Chapter 1, evidence of American Indian poverty is so overwhelming that few observers would dispute the contention that some may respond aggressively. One of the most visible signs of deprivation is reservation housing. Although living conditions vary considerably, running water, central heating, indoor plumbing, and electricity are not always present. Unemployment and impoverished living conditions are often a way of life for American Indians. Although urban Indians have a greater probability of finding work than do those residing on reservations, they are most often restricted to blue-collar jobs, if they find work at all, and still frequently live in substandard housing (Sorkin, 1976, 1978).

The helplessness and humiliation that are often associated with being poor were revealed many times during the course of these interviews. Many spoke angrily of the economic oppression their people had experienced and continue to experience today. It is not difficult to understand how some may engage in aggressive activity as the result of living in a society where many devalue them as a people and provide few economic opportunities—particularly on reservations. While some had been employed at various times in their lives, they all went through long periods of unemployment. Further, most were underemployed, if employed at all. However, even though high levels of unemployment existed among these men, the cultural norm of "providing for your family" was prevalent as well. With the structural reality of little economic opportunity and the cultural norm of "paternal support" existing within the same context, it is not surprising that feelings of inadequacy and frustration could emerge and perhaps even lead to violent behavior. Respondent eleven explains:

> I have always been the type of person who felt like you got what you deserved. I never was one to line up in a line and wait for food. That's the way I still feel. It's pretty hard to put that in perspective when you can't find a job—you can't put food on the table. Did I deserve this—you start hating yourself.

Another offender states, "A man is supposed to be able to provide for his family, and here I was, not even able to find a job with two kids to feed. You know I felt worthless except when I was drunk—then I didn't feel nothing." Respondent six recalls what it was like growing up in poverty and facing the reality of unemployment on the reservation:

> I didn't even realize we were poor until I got older—like 10 or 11. I started looking around. And you know it wasn't as bad because almost everyone else was poor, too, but when I got old enough to care, you realized that there was not a damn thing you could do about it. No jobs—nothing. Shit people don't realize. There is no such things as paper routes on the res—there is nothing. You're into bad shit before you know it.

Many offenders described feelings of helplessness when they were not able to provide for their families or girlfriends. Some had trouble holding down a job because of alcohol abuse. Others experienced discrimination in obtaining employment and on the job. One described his excitement at finally getting a job as a gas station attendant, but then he was fired one day out of the blue because another guy who had worked there for a long time "didn't like working with an Indian."

On the reservation, employment opportunities are often seasonal, if available at all. Respondent nineteen explains some of the problems encountered with seasonal and sporadic employment:

> For purely economic reasons I started stealing. I did have work and I made pretty good money, but when we ran out of work, I had debts. You know on the reservation a lot of work is seasonal, and so when you are making money, you buy things but don't think about what will pay the bills when the job is gone. I first stole some copper wire from the phone company, and when the cops were after me, I stole a car to get the hell out of "Dodge"—it snowballs pretty fast after that. The next thing you know I'm in here for killing someone when I was stealing from his house.

Although some respondents linked being poor with their induction into the world of crime, others merely reflected on the frustrations they experienced. One offender described these frustrations vividly and how such emotional states can lead to violence:

> Without a job you sit in your house day after day—nothing to do. You listen to that same car drive by your house again and again, and pretty soon you hate those people in that car. Kids go running through your yard—back and forth and back and forth—and pretty soon you hate those kids. Pretty soon you want to hurt somebody.

Narratives such as this are compelling evidence for including economic deprivation in any theoretical guide for American Indian homicide.

Any discussion of American Indian homicide would not be complete without including alcohol/drug use. The next section will explore alcohol and drug use in the lives of these offenders and the role that this use played in the homicide.

Alcohol/Drug Use

> One of the things that I am doing now is trying to get off alcohol because it is one of the things that brought me here. It was really bad. For many years I was hooked on booze. I have put the stuff down in here. There were times in my life before prison when I put it down, too, but not for very long because it was always around. Alcohol destroyed my family. It wasn't that my parents didn't love us, but they had a special place in their hearts for booze, too. The booze tore us all up. It shattered everything—all of the dreams that we had, all of

the love—everything that we shared as far as kinship was destroyed by booze. (Respondent twelve)

The Indian Health Service believes that no other condition adversely affects as many aspects of Indian life in the United States as alcoholism does. Whittaker (1982) investigated the incidence of alcohol consumption on a midwestern reservation and found that alcohol problems directly or indirectly affected almost the entire reservation population and that approximately one of every three Indians over fifteen years of age drank to excess. Further, among young adult Indians (particularly males), the incidence of excessive drinking was close to 95 percent.[10] While alarmingly high, such incidence rates have been documented to primarily affect only young American Indians. In his review of the literature on alcohol abuse among American Indians, May (1989) concludes that although more Indian youths drink heavily than do non-Indian youths, this trend reverses in adulthood. American Indians who are thirty years old and above appear to have a rate of drinking below the U.S. average.

For the homicide offenders interviewed here, alcohol abuse was a primary contributor to their violence. As indicated in Table 3.1, all but one of the homicide offenses were committed under the influence of alcohol or drugs. This high rate of alcohol consumption before the commission of violence has been documented in the American Indian population by others as well.[11]

Almost all the respondents acknowledged the problem of alcohol abuse in relation to either themselves or their people. One offender stated, "Alcohol and drugs separate the brotherhood we could have. You know we want to have all these things in here like pow wows, but we can't because we spend all the money on drugs and alcohol. It ruins us outside of this hole and continues to ruin us inside here." One respondent reminisced:

> My grandfather told me once, if you take a look around us, there's one thing that's going to destroy us, and that's alcohol. There's another thing that's going to destroy us, and that's poverty. And there's another thing and that's people claiming to be what they're not. I look around now and I see it. One of the things that brought me here [to prison] was alcohol.

Others talked of stealing property to get money to buy alcohol and drugs. "We were breaking into houses, fighting people—doing anything to get more money. Anything so we could get our next drink."

It is certain that alcohol was a contributing factor in the lives of each of the offenders interviewed. What is not so certain, however, is why the influence of alcohol leads some to engage in violence and others to be passive.[12] MacAndrew and Edgerton (1970) believe that aggressive reactions to alcohol are learned, rather than being a function of "toxically disinhibited brains operating in impulse-driven bodies" (p. 165). Specifically, these authors state, "the way people comport themselves when they are drunk is determined not by alcohol's toxic assault upon the seat of moral judgment, conscience, or the like, but by what their society makes of and imparts to them concerning the state of drunkenness." These authors make a very powerful case that violence is a learned reaction to alcohol (even though it is certainly not a universal response among American Indians). Through a content analysis of the diaries of missionaries and fur traders, MacAndrew and Edgerton document how the Indian came to see that "changes-for-the-worse" were to be expected during drunkenness, "for at such times the drinker was temporarily inhabited by an evil supernatural agent." These authors find many citations that do not portray the Indian's first contact with alcohol as resulting in drunken brawls and mayhem; rather, many Indians reacted in fear or passivity. By watching the White man, however, the Indian soon learned what behavior alcohol should produce. MacAndrew and Edgerton state:

And from this, the Indian reached the entirely reasonable conclusion that since he was thus "possessed," his actions when drunk were not his own and he was not responsible for them. After all, the Indians precontact cultures already contained an ample of time out ceremonies and supernatural agents (e.g., witchcraft, dreams, spirit possession, etc.) under whose influence a man became less than strictly responsible for his own actions. What is more, the notion that the state of drunkenness was excusing of those transgressions committed while "under the influence" was entirely consonant with the model the white man provided, for in regard to his own drunken transgressions and those of his fellows, the white man, too, ignored much and forgave still more on the grounds that when drunk, one is "under the influence." So vivid were the examples of drunken mayhem and so well did such changes-for-the-worse mesh with precontact notions that it is difficult to imagine how a consciously conceived program of instruction about alcohol's "influence" on conduct could possibly have improved on the "lesson plan" that the Indian's white tutors provided. (p. 149)

Evidence of this learned response to alcohol was also found in the narratives of the offenders in this study. One man told of witnessing his parents fight after drinking as a child. "I remember watching my parents getting drunk on weekends—things would usually end up in a fight. My brothers and sisters and I just sat on the bunk bed and watched. Like I said, when you see, when you hear, you start to act like the person you're not supposed to be." The early process through which many learned this response to alcohol was most often vicarious rather than direct, as indicated by the above quote.

Some described how the anger and frustrations experienced in every-day life would easily surface and result in violence under the influence of alcohol.

> If you get mad at someone sometime but don't do anything about it—you know like if someone pissed you off a few days earlier and then one night you get drunk—you go after him. I don't know. It's like you have the guts or something. Everything comes up—all of the anger. Sometimes you get angry at people you're not even angry at—you sometimes take all of your anger out on anyone that's around.

> All alcohol does is provoke violence. It's like a false courage, you know? There is the anger in you because of the society you live in and just the everyday shit. Where we live builds up frustration and anger; but when you are straight and everything, you won't show that—you will more likely turn the other cheek. As soon as you start drinking alcohol, it just enhances all that anger. You say. "I remember this guy did me wrong, I'm gonna kick his ass." It's false courage.

It is easy to understand how frustrations and anger might easily surface during a drinking episode and how this same drinking could sometimes be used as an excuse for violent outbursts. Of course, some offenders in this study used drunkenness as an excuse for committing homicide. And why not? Even our legal system can be more lenient if one was "under the influence" during the commission of a crime than if one was not. In the extreme, four respondents maintained that they had blacked out and had no recollection of the killing, while six others remembered only parts of the incident.

> You know when I woke up in jail the last time and I asked them what I did, I couldn't believe it. Killed someone. I couldn't believe it. You know, first forgery, then robbery, now this. If drinking in a bar one night is going to cause this, I don't want to do it anymore. You know it's not like I'm smart enough to know better—but it's been a contin-ual process. One thing after the other—all after I had been drinking.

Others talked about the personality transformation that occurred after they had been drinking. "I'm a different person when I drink. I go crazy. Who the hell am I—I don't know." Other offenders did not use the drink-ing as an excuse; they simply acknowledged it as a sad reality of their lives.

SUMMARY

Most of the homicide offenders interviewed were born into a cycle of poverty—blocked from legitimate economic opportunities and forced into dependency. For many, the distress of this situation was compounded by family disruption and disorganization. Feelings of frustration and powerlessness emerged early in the lives of these offenders. Solace from these feelings was often found in a "bottle" or in other drugs. The alcohol/drug dependency only exacerbated other situational conditions, rendering many unable to hold down a job or keep their families together.

Some adopted an aggressive identity, thus restoring the sense of manhood that was not otherwise attainable through economic success. Rewards were obtained from acts of bravery—not from "A's" in math or acceptance into college. These ideals of "masculine prowess" were essentially the same, whether staged in the rural isolation of the reservation or in the ghettos of an urban area.

The adoption of this value system that condones violence was not necessary for some to kill, however. Some may have been propelled by the frustrations produced by structural circumstances alone. It is true that not all American Indians who are born into conditions of poverty are propelled to commit murder. Many go on to college and make their way into the middle class. Nor is it true that all Indian children born to alcoholic parents and dysfunctional families are destined to a life of crime. When conditions such as these are coupled with values that condone the use of violence and alcohol, however, their contribution to homicide seems to be exponential.

Much of the learning that enabled the offenders to cope with these structural and cultural conditions seems to have come through vicarious processes, such as witnessing parents or other significant others. One respondent stated, "It's how you learn to cope—how you learn to manage the tension and frustration in life. It's the way I saw people handling problems—with their fists and with alcohol."

Another element of the social learning process that they verbalized was the great effect that reinforcement provided. Much of this reinforcement was in the form of acceptance by one's peer group. Also inherent in this contingency was the fact that ostracism was the punishment often experienced by a youth not willing to participate in such deviant acts as drinking or stealing.

> Just like on the reservation. Everyone is just trying to be like the next guy. Everyone else is getting drunk. Why not me? Everyone else is having a party. Why not me? And if you don't—you don't fit in. People give you shit. Even if you have white friends, people give you shit.

The process of learning these behaviors is important. As one offender recalls, "I got involved in a group when I was seven or eight. They were stealing stuff and I learned quick and I learned well. Before that I had never even stolen a piece of bubble gum before. But when I learned how, I was good."

Another offender revealed the prevalence of such activity on the reservation, thus limiting the options one had for reinforcement and acceptance by nondeviant peers:

> It amounts to just getting in with the wrong crowd. I started drinking at 13 and taking drugs a year later. I guess it's not just the wrong crowd that's the problem—there isn't many other crowds to choose from. You just do what everybody else is doing or you don't have any friends.

Another quote reveals that the power of ostracism and banishment from a group as a form of punishment is just as strong in the prison setting:

> I've been in treatment for 5 weeks and I'm doing good, but I'm so scared to get back in the population. I want to transfer to another treatment that's longer. Maybe then I will really be strong enough. You know like six weeks and I'm a changed person—fuck that—I'm not. I'm doing good now because I have support to do good, but put me back out with the people that are saying, "here, bro, want to get high" or whatever, you know, and it won't last. I need to really get stable on the inside because it's just on the surface now. Otherwise I won't be able to say no, especially when you'll get shit for not doing it—not going along. I'll fall back into the same old shit. It's not easy not going along with the group—especially in here.

When an individual's only means of reinforcement is derived from a peer group that encourages alcohol and drug use, one can see the difficulty that individual has in trying to abstain. This is consistent with Akers' (1985) social learning theory of deviance. He posits that one of the ways in which a person learns deviant behavior is through the effective and available reinforcers he or she receives from significant others for behaving in certain ways—in this case, deviantly. When an individual receives negative stimuli or punishment for not engaging in deviant behavior, it would be almost impossible for that individual to get straight, even if such opportunities (i.e., treatment and counseling facilities) existed.

It should also be noted that models were provided not only within an individual's family and peers, but through authority figures as well. Images abound in our culture that support the use of violence, and even glorify it. These images can have a tremendous impact, particularly when they are validated with real-life experiences. One offender offered tremendous insight into this:

> Little Indian kids see violence all the time. They are used to seeing an Indian person beat up on the street by cops for no apparent reason. It's not right. Then when they grow, they might be subjected to the

same treatment. If authority figures are abusive, what's to stop them from being violent, too? And when they get drunk, the chance of violence happening is greater. They see this outside the home, then they sometimes see it at home.

The theoretical guide of American Indian homicide that emerges from the interview narratives combines elements of social disorganization, economic deprivation, a subculture of violence, culture conflict, perceived powerlessness, and the intervening variables of alcohol and drug use. To be complete the model also includes the antecedent variable of internal colonialism.

Although this guide represents multiple factors, other variables may also contribute to the high rate of American Indian homicide. For example, inadequate medical resources may escalate a case of assault to a case of homicide.[13] Discriminatory imposition of the law may also contribute.[14] Chapter five will outline these alternative explanations in greater detail.

It is not suggested that this guide of American Indian homicide is definitive. Nevertheless, using these theoretical concepts as reference points is essential to proceed with the empirical testing in the next chapter.

NOTES

1. Levy & Kuntz, 1969; Ogden, Spector & Hill, 1970; Westermeyer & Brantner, 1972; Frederick, 1973; Kraus & Buffler, 1979; Humphrey & Kupferer, 1982.

2. Wolfgang & Ferracuti, 1967; Hackney, 1969; Gastil, 1971; Messner, 1982, 1983; Huff-Corzine, Corzine, & Moore, 1986; Baron & Straus, 1989.

3. Loftin & Hill, 1974; Blau & Blau, 1982; Williams, 1984; Parker & Loftin, 1985; Sampson, 1985; Williams & Flewelling, 1988.

4. Peyote use was restricted by the United States Supreme Court in *Employment Division v. Smith*, 1990.

5. Brown, 1970; Harvard Encyclopedia of American Ethnic Groups, 1980; Deloria, 1985.

6. See Unger, 1977, for a detailed account.

7. This is an excerpt from an unpublished report entitled, "An Equal Chance: Handbook for Counseling Indian Students" developed by Barbara A. Farlow, Assistant Director of Extended Services at Wisconsin State University, Stevens Point.

8. Curlee, 1969; Resnik & Dizmang, 1971; Frederick, 1973; May, 1975; Hockhirchen & Jilek, 1985; Berlin, 1987.

9. For general theoretical discussions of economic sources of crime see Merton, 1957; Cloward & Ohlin, 1960; Clinard, 1964; and Braithwaite, 1979. Empirical support for a link between economic deprivation and homicide is offered by many investigators including Loftin & Hill, 1974; Smith & Parker,

1980; Blau & Blau,1982; Messner, 1982, 1983a, 1983b; Williams, 1984; Sampson, 1985; and Williams & Flewelling, 1988.

10. For other incidence studies, see Curlee, 1969; Resnik & Dizmang, 1971; and May, 1975.

11. Kraus & Buffler, 1979; Broudy & May, 1983; Weisner, Weibel-Orlando, & Long, 1984; and Lex, 1987.

12. For a detailed review of the literature which investigates the etiology of American Indian drinking, see May, 1977.

13. Doerner, 1983; Williams & Bachman, 1988.

14. Swigert & Farrel, 1977.

A Statistical Analysis of American Indian Homicide: A Test of Social Disorganization and Economic Deprivation at the Reservation County and State Levels

While the previous chapter examined the etiology of American Indian homicide at the individual level, the remainder of our analysis will examine the correlates of homicide rates at both the reservation and the state levels. Remember that Chapter 2 documented homicide rates at the national level. While American Indian rates were shown to be alarmingly high, these rates when disaggregated to reservation and state levels, illuminate a problem much more severe. Tables 4.1 and 4.4 display state- and reservation-county-level American Indian homicide rates, respectively. For the state level, homicide rates were calculated only for states that contained reservations. From this, you can see that more than ten states—including South Dakota, Wyoming, Nebraska, Minnesota, Wisconsin, and Arizona—have American Indian homicide rates over 10 per 100,000 population, with some states reaching rates over 40 per 100,000 population. Further, as shown in Table 4.4, some reservation counties have homicide rates that are over 100 per 100,000 population. This chapter will investigate the structural conditions present on reservations and in states that may contribute to these high rates of lethal violence.

The selection of theoretical constructs tested in this analysis was guided by the model of American Indian homicide developed in Chapter 3. Reiterating, the model combines elements of social disorganization, economic deprivation, a subculture of violence, and culture conflict and perceived powerlessness, as well as an intervening variable of alcohol/drug abuse. Also included in the model is the antecedent variable of internal colonialism. This individual-level model has corresponding aggregate-level interpretations. Because of limited data availability, however, this chapter evaluates elements of this model at the aggregate level only when suitable indicators were available. Specifically, this research focuses on two elements in the model: social disorganization and economic deprivation. Before continuing, however, I will reacquaint the reader with the foundations on which each of these theoretical constructs is based.

THEORETICAL RATIONALE

Social Disorganization

The foundation for the social disorganization perspective originates from one of Durkheim's early arguments that rapid social change is associated with increases in crime due to the breakdown of social controls. It later emerged in the writings and research of sociologists at the University of Chicago.[1]

While there is no single definition of social disorganization that all adhere to, the term is generally used to describe conditions that undermine the ability of traditional institutions to govern social behavior (Baron & Straus, 1989; Skogan, 1989). Skogan (1989) notes that while America's past is riddled with such things as illiteracy, cyclical unemployment, and low wages, crime rates tend to remain low where traditional agents of social control (i.e., the family, schools, traditional values, and so on) remain strong. He concludes that "Crime problems became worse when those agents lost their hold on the young" (p. 244).

Investigators in the comparative homicide tradition have also advanced social disorganization to explain the partial variation that exists in homicide differentials between aggregate units (e.g., states, cities) in this country (Blau & Blau, 1982; Crutchfield, Geerken, & Grove, 1982; Wilkinson, 1984; Williams & Flewelling, 1989). In American Indian communities, this social disorganization is manifested in many forms, including the breakup of families and the high rates of geographical mobility of reservation citizens between urban areas and the reservation and also from reservation to reservation. This chapter will empirically assess the extent to which reservation county-to-county and state-to-state differences in the level of social disorganization are associated with corresponding differences in American Indian homicide.

Economic Deprivation

The psychological consequences of being poor are many. It engenders hopelessness, apathy, and anger. To reiterate from the last chapter, one form of coping with the alienation and hostility that poverty may produce is through aggression. Williams and Flewelling (1988) maintain that conditions of extreme scarcity can create a host of manifestations such as "powerlessness and brutalization" which can, in turn, "provoke physical aggression in conflict situations" (p. 423).

As the last chapter revealed, virtually all of the homicide offenders interviewed for this research were unemployed at the time of the homicide. Further, virtually all of their annual incomes fell below the Social Security Administration's poverty level the year prior to the offense. In addition, virtually all of the studies that examine the etiology of homicide across geographical locales find empirical evidence supporting the economic deprivation–homicide link.[2] For these reasons, we will also assess the extent to which reservation county-to-county and state-to-state differences in levels of economic deprivation are associated with corresponding differences in American Indian homicide.

This chapter will investigate two research hypotheses:

1. The higher the level of social disorganization within an American Indian community, the higher the level of lethal violence.
2. The higher the level of economic deprivation within an American Indian community, the higher the level of lethal violence.

The remainder of the chapter will be divided into two sections. The first will present an analysis of American Indian homicide at the state level. The second will concentrate on American Indian homicide at the reservation county level. Each section will be prefaced by a discussion of the methods specific to the unit of analysis investigated therein.

STATE-LEVEL ANALYSIS

This section will present a multivariate analysis of American Indian homicide using states as the units of analysis. Although some have questioned the validity of states as homogeneous entities (Loftin & Hill, 1974), others have advocated their use (Straus, 1985). I believe a case can be made, however, for the use of states as the unit of analysis for an American Indian–specific analysis. First, the American Indian population primarily lives either in the reservation setting or in urban areas. Although both life situations might provide different cultural and structural experiences at the individual level, some researchers have found that American Indian mortality in both locations is often similar, with reservation Indians experiencing significantly higher mortality rates only in certain age groups (Kenen S. Hammerslough, 1987).

Reservation and urban living situations are not so cut and dried, however. Many young adult Indians have high mobility rates between urban areas and the reservation. In fact, all of the homicide offenders interviewed for this research moved back and forth between the two geographic locations an average of 1.7 times annually before incarceration. This does not include visits between the two areas, but rather actual relocations. Gundlach and Roberts (1978) explain that "poverty has motivated many young Indians to leave reservations for cities where, often times, subsequent failure has pushed them back to their secure, albeit poor, reservation communities."

Because of this mobility issue, the use of states as units of analysis provides the most appropriate way to capture the influence of cultural and structural variables on aggregate homicide rates beyond specific reservation-level analyses.

Methods

Because this analysis was performed *only* on states where reservations are located, it is limited to twenty-seven states.[3] This was done because many of the nonreservation states revealed homicide rates of zero; also, a few states had very high rates simply because they had a very small American Indian population, thereby making them suspect for small sample variability. Although it would be preferable to have a large number of states available for multivariate analysis, homicide is a rare crime in the first place. This fact, along with small Indian populations in some states, may yield questionable rates in several states.

Theoretical Indicators

Economic Deprivation. The indicator used to measure economic deprivation was a two-item index composed of the percentage of American Indian families that fell below the poverty level (U.S. Bureau of the Census, 1980) and the percentage of the American Indian population that was unemployed (*The World Almanac*, 1988). State rankings of this variable are provided in Table 4.1.

Social Disorganization. The divorce rate was used in this analysis as an indicator of social disorganization (U.S. Bureau of the Census, 1980). Although it would be preferable to use a multi-item indicator like the one used in the next section, American Indian–specific data were limited on the state level. However, many studies have utilized the single item of divorce to represent levels of social disorganization present in social systems (Blau & Blau, 1982; Williams & Flewelling, 1988). As Blau and Blau (1982) state, "Disproportionate numbers of divorced and separated in a population may be indicative of much instability, disorientation, and conflict in personal relations" (p. 124).

Controls. In addition to the above theoretical indicators, the percentages of Blacks, urban residents, and American Indians between the ages of eighteen and twenty-four were included as demographic controls in the

Table 4.1

State-Level Rank Order Listings of American Indian Unemployment, Poverty, Divorce, and Homicide Rates (*N* = 27 States)

RANK	STATE	UNEMPLOYMENT	STATE	POVERTY RATE	STATE	DIVORCE RATE	STATE	HOMICIDE RATE
1	IOW	66.00	S D	45.80	FLA	282.79	ALK	47.32
2	WYO	65.00	ARI	40.20	TEN	267.50	IOW	31.17
3	S D	64.00	N D	39.10	GA	248.86	ILL	22.98
4	NEB	60.00	VT	39.10	IND	242.25	NEB	19.03
5	MIN	59.00	N M	37.60	KY	240.48	N C	18.88
6	MIC	58.00	R I	34.00	MO	240.33	MIN	18.56
7	N Y	56.00	UTH	31.50	OH	233.79	ORG	14.07
8	CAL	55.00	MON	30.90	ARK	222.23	MO	12.53
9	WAS	52.00	NEB	30.70	ALK	212.22	S C	12.31
10	ALK	51.00	IDA	29.70	ALA	211.54	WAS	11.96
11	N D	50.00	MIS	29.60	VT	191.12	CON	11.29
12	WIS	49.00	D C	28.80	ILL	188.63	COL	11.07
13	COL	47.00	IOW	28.10	W V	187.78	KAN	11.03
14	IDA	46.00	MIN	28.00	WYO	187.05	HAW	10.00
15	NEV	44.00	ME	27.10	ORG	184.46	MD	9.92
16	ARI	43.00	N C	25.40	CAL	182.76	MON	9.42
17	MON	39.00	TEN	24.40	HAW	182.30	WYO	9.40
18	N C	39.00	PA	24.10	ME	179.44	N Y	9.33
19	ORG	37.00	KY	23.10	NEV	178.27	WIS	9.22
20	N M	32.00	WAS	22.90	S C	176.88	CAL	9.07
21	FLA	26.00	WIS	22.50	IOW	174.52	OKL	8.87
22	KAN	26.00	MAS	22.40	CON	173.55	N J	7.64
23	MIS	26.00	ALA	22.20	COL	169.56	IDA	7.30
24	UTH	25.00	S C	21.50	WAS	168.67	VA	6.90
25	ME	22.00	N Y	21.20	DEL	168.32	NEV	6.76
26	LA	18.00	ALK	20.10	KAN	168.26	N M	6.38
27	OKL	18.00	OKL	19.90	PA	164.72	PA	6.33

following analysis. The percentage of the Indian population aged eighteen to twenty-four is included not only because this age range reflects the highest homicide rate in the population as a whole, but also because the age concentration of American Indians is greater in these younger years than for the equivalent age cohort in the total U.S. population.

Homicide Rates

The homicide data analyzed in this chapter were obtained from the Supplementary Homicide Report collected by the Federal Bureau of Investigation as a part of its Uniform Crime Reporting program. The entire data set was compiled at the University of New Hampshire and is referred to as the Comparative Homicide File (CHF) (Williams and Flewelling, 1987). Among these incidents of homicide, the sample is restricted to one-on-one cases and covers the entire 1980-1984 period, not individual years. This procedure was used to reduce the influence of random aberrations in year-to-year estimates, in addition to preventing unreliable rates based on low frequencies. Using weighting and adjustment procedures for missing data, the total homicide rates were calculated as follows:

$$\text{Homicide rate} = [(I/P) \times 100,000]/5$$

where I = the total number of weighted and adjusted incidents of murder and nonnegligent manslaughter and P = the total American Indian population of a state. The division by five indicates that the rates are calculated over the entire 1980-1984 period and then expressed on a per-year basis. For a detailed description of the rate calculation procedure, see Williams and Flewelling (1987). The first column of Table 4.1 provides the ranking of each state on the basis of its American Indian homicide rate.

Transformations

In empirical research, there is no reason to assume that the relationships among every set of variables will be linear. In some cases, curvilinear regression analysis can provide a better understanding of empirical relationships than can any linear model. This is the case with these data.

Preliminary univariate analyses of several of the variables used in this chapter revealed severe skewness. Skewed distributions often resemble symmetrical distributions with one whole side of the distribution pulled either upward or downward. This results not only in a string of extreme values on one side of the distribution, but also in a mean that is either pulled higher or lower, depending on whether the skewness is in the negative or positive direction. All American Indian–specific variables used in this analysis were positively skewed. In addition to these statistical concerns, previous comparative research has shown that the relationships between the total homicide rate and other variables, such as percentage of poor, are nonlinear and must therefore be adjusted logarithmically (Williams, 1984).

Hartwig and Dearing (1979) state that "nonnormality and nonlinearity often go hand in hand and, because of this, reexpression is a useful response to both problems" (p. 54). For these reasons, all variables in the analysis that follows have been reexpressed in logarithmic form (base 10). This reexpression simply uses a logged numeric scale instead of the original measurement of the variable.

Tests were also performed to detect possible problems with multicollinearity and heteroskedasticity. These tests revealed that there are no serious threats of either condition being present in this analysis.

Results

Table 4.2 displays the bivariate relationships between all exogenous and endogenous variables. The strongest correlation is between American Indian unemployment and American Indian homicide (.42), with percent Indian and percent of Indian population between the ages of fifteen and twenty-four following with correlations of .23 and .26, respectively. But before conclusions can be made regarding these relationships, we must use the multivariate statistical technique of regression. From this, we will then be able to determine the extent to which each of these variables is related to American Indian homicide, while controlling for all other variables.

Table 4.3 displays the regression analysis esimating the American Indian homicide rate using these same independent variables. This equation resulted in an adjusted R-squared of .28. From this table, we can see that only American Indian poverty is significant when predicting Indian homicide.

Thus, using these theoretical indicators, it appears that only economic deprivation is a significant predictor of American Indian homicide differentials among states, net of the other theoretical indicators included in this analysis.

Table 4.2
Correlation Matrix of the Total American Indian Homicide Rate and All American Indian–Specific Independent Variables
(N = 27 States)

	1	2	3	4	5	6
1. AMER. INDIAN HOMICIDE	–					
2. AMER. INDIAN UNEMPLOYMNT	.42	–				
3. AMER. INDIAN DIVORCE	.05	-.01	–			
4. AMER. INDIAN AGED 15–24	.26	.08	.56	–		
5. AMER. INDIAN %POOR	-.14	.11	-.69	-.40	–	
6. PERCENT AMER. INDIAN	.23	.07	-.48	-.07	.46	–

Table 4.3
Regression Analysis of the American Indian Homicide Rate
with Five American Indian–Specific Independent Variables
(N = 27 States)

Independent Variables	b	SE(b)	beta	t
AMER.INDIAN UNEMPLOYMNT	1.17	.494	.427	2.36*
AMER.INDIAN DIVORCE	-.42	.808	-.158	-.527
AMER.INDIAN AGED 15-24	.870	.971	.202	.897
AMER.INDIAN %POOR	-1.24	.928	-.336	-1.33
PERCENT AMER.INDIAN	.254	.199	.271	1.27

* = 1-tailed significance: $p = .05$

RESERVATION COUNTY–LEVEL ANALYSIS

The remainder of this chapter will focus specifically on explaining reservation-to-reservation differences in homicide. While reservations are logically part of the state-level analysis performed above, we cannot definitively extrapolate the hypotheses stated in the beginning of this chapter to reservations without analyzing data obtained exclusively from reservations. The task here is to assess the degree to which structural circumstances, such as social disorganization and economic deprivation, increase or decrease homicide rates in reservation communities.

Methods

The analysis performed in this section relies on data from 114 counties that were all or partially located on reservation land. County-level independent variables were obtained from the Census Subject Reports of American Indians, Eskimos, and Aleuts on Identified Reservations and in the Historic Areas of Oklahoma (U.S. Bureau of the Census, 1980). This Census report contained many more variables specific to American Indians than were available for the state-level analysis. This allowed indexes to be constructed that were designed to measure the degrees of both instability and poverty within reservation communities. These data were then matched to American Indian homicide rates, which were calculated from county-level data obtained from the Indian Health Service in the Department of Health and Human Services for the years 1980 to 1987.

Theoretical Indicators

Social Disorganization. A two-indicator social disorganization index designed to measure the degree of instability in reservation communities was constructed. The index includes measures of geographical mobility and female-headed households.

The two specific indicators included in the index are (1) the percentage of American Indian families who are female-headed with no husband and with children under the age of eighteen and (2) the percentage of American Indians who did not live on the same reservation in 1979 or 1980. Both of these variables were selected because previous research provides empirical evidence and a theoretical rationale for their contribution to the instability of society.

Research suggests that "single mother families are less likely to become rooted in a stable residence and social network and are more apt to find themselves overburdened with the competing demands of family and work" (Baron & Straus, 1989, p. 138). Further evidence is offered by Skogan (1989), who notes that indicators of the extent of family disorganization, including female-headed households, are strongly related to neighborhoods levels of crime. Based on this empirical support and on the assumption that inordinate strains on female-headed families might contribute to a climate of social instability, this indicator was included in this index of social disorganization.

The mobility rate within a community has also been documented to be related to homicide and other criminal activity.[4] The theoretical rationale for including this indicator is that change in the residential population diminishes the sense of attachment to community norms and reduces the ability of established institutions to regulate social behavior.

Construction of this index was a simple additive procedure, in which the z scores of both indicators were added into an index and then this sum was retransformed into a z-score index. This index was created to capture as many different spheres of social disorganization as possible with the data available. The fifth column in Table 4.4 lists the counties in rank order based on this index.

Economic Deprivation. An index intended to measure the extent of economic deprivation in reservation counties was constructed in the same manner described above. This index includes (1) the percentage of American Indian families below the Social Security Administration's

Table 4.4
Reservation-County-Level Rank Order Listings of the American Indian Homicide Rate, the Social Disorganization Index, and the Poverty Index (*N* = 120 Reservation Counties)

RANK	COUNTY	ST	HOMICIDE RATE	COUNTY	ST	SOCIAL DISORG.	COUNTY	ST	POVERTY INDEX
1	Bingham	ID	6.41	Klickitat	WASH	-2.16	Klickitat	WASH	.
2	Franklin	NY	6.74	PrinceofWales	AK	-1.91	Tuolumne	CA	.
3	PrinceofWales	AK	8.21	Sonoma	CA	-1.71	Yellowstone	MONT	.
4	Montezuma	CO	8.32	Pondera	MONT	-1.61	DelNorte	CA	.
5	Cattaraugus	NY	8.43	Franklin	NY	-1.58	Day	SD	.
6	Dewey	SD	8.70	King	WASH	-1.49	Kootnai	ID	.
7	CarsonCity	NEV	9.36	SanJuan	UT	-1.23	Wood	WIS	.
8	Elko	NEV	9.46	Jackson	NC	-1.23	Brown	KS	-2.27
9	NezPerce	ID	9.82	Brown	WIS	-1.23	PrinceofWales	AK	-1.87
10	DelNorte	CA	10.43	SanJuan	NM	-1.23	Osage	OK	-1.52
11	Tulare	CA	10.92	Leake	MISS	-1.20	Stevens	WASH	-1.43
12	Taos	NM	11.13	Glacier	MONT	-1.19	LaPlata	CO	-1.37
13	Brown	WIS	11.18	Navajo	AZ	-1.18	Ashland	WIS	-1.35
14	Yavopai	AZ	11.27	Coconino	AZ	-1.14	RioAriba	NM	-1.35
15	Sonoma	CA	11.75	Valencia	NM	-1.11	Washoe	NEV	-1.34
16	GraysHarbor	WASH	11.89	Glades	FL	-1.10	Jackson	KC	-1.33
17	MCKinley	NM	12.72	Mason	WASH	-1.01	Elko	NEV	-1.31
18	Ashland	WIS	12.81	Otero	NM	-.94	NezPerce	ID	-1.28
19	Lake	MONT	12.87	Elko	NEV	-.94	Brouward	FL	-1.27
20	Washington	ME	13.14	MCKinley	NM	-.93	CarsonCity	NEV	-1.24
21	Snohomish	WASH	13.17	Apache	AZ	-.92	Mohave	AZ	-1.23
22	Menominee	WIS	13.58	Montezuma	CO	-.90	Ferry	WASH	-1.13
23	Mahnomen	MINN	13.59	Mohave	AZ	-.87	Outagamie	WIS	-1.12
24	Ferry	WASH	14.09	Ferry	WASH	-.87	Taos	NM	-1.09
25	SanJuan	NM	15.68	Bernalillo	NM	-.84	Inyo	CA	-1.05
26	Washoe	NEV	15.77	Sauk	WIS	-.81	Burnett	WIS	-1.04

#	County	State	Value
27	CharlesMix	SD	15.97
28	Coconino	AZ	16.07
29	Whatcom	WASH	16.81
30	SanJuan	UT	17.01
31	Mendocino	CA	17.16
32	Outagamie	WIS	17.26
33	Rolette	ND	17.27
34	Benson	ND	17.34
35	Osage	OK	17.54
36	Clark	NEV	18.33
37	Stevens	WASH	18.39
38	Mohave	AZ	18.59
39	Apache	AZ	19.04
40	St.Louis	MINN	19.40
41	Graham	AZ	20.23
42	Riverside	CA	21.06
43	BigHorn	MONT	21.14
44	Okanogan	WASH	21.21
45	Humboldt	NEV	21.32
46	Navajo	AZ	21.42
47	Brown	KS	21.84
48	Bannock	ID	22.37
49	Pierce	WASH	22.84
50	Bernalillo	NM	22.92
51	Jackson	NC	22.93
52	Tuolumne	CA	23.38
53	Hill	MONT	23.43
54	Becker	MINN	23.59
55	Pima	AZ	23.83
56	Skagit	WASH	24.44
57	LaPlata	CO	24.72
58	RioAriba	NM	25.72
59	Beltrami	MN	27.53
60	Jackson	KS	27.97
61	Thurston	NEB	28.23
62	Neshoba	MISS	28.47
63	Klickitat	WASH	28.98
64	Humboldt	CA	29.14
65	Mountrail	ND	29.39

County	State	Value
Bannock	ID	.76
Marshall	SD	.74
Swain	NC	.72
RioAriba	NM	.68
Taos	NM	.68
Polk	WIS	.68
Gila	AZ	.66
Mahnomen	MINN	.63
BigHorn	MONT	.61
Tuolumne	CA	.59
Menominee	WIS	.59
Graham	AZ	.56
Fremont	WY	.52
Cattaraugus	NY	.50
Hendry	FL	.50
Yuma	AZ	.48
Neshoba	MISS	.48
Uintah	UT	.45
Whatcom	WASH	.44
Pinal	AZ	.42
Stevens	WASH	.41
Osage	OK	.40
Jefferson	OR	.39
Jackson	KS	.33
Dewey	SD	.31
Lake	MONT	.30
Hill	MONT	.29
Koochiching	MINN	.29
Blaine	MONT	.28
GraysHarbor	WASH	.27
Missoula	MONT	.27
Rolette	ND	.25
Becker	MINN	.20
Shannon	SD	.18
Outagamie	WIS	.18
Wasco	OR	.11
Rosebud	MONT	.08
Roosevelt	MONT	.04
Yakima	WASH	.04

County	State	Value
Leake	MISS	.94
Nye	NEV	.93
Thurston	NEB	.92
Umatilla	OR	.90
Idaho	ID	.86
Douglas	NEV	.70
Franklin	NY	.66
Neshoba	MISS	.64
Brown	WIS	.63
Sonoma	CA	.59
Wasco	OR	.57
BigHorn	MONT	.55
Knox	NEB	.52
Uintah	UT	.50
McLean	ND	.45
GraysHarbor	WASH	.41
Menominee	WIS	.40
Bernalillo	NM	.38
Jefferson	OR	.37
SanJuan	NM	.35
Humboldt	CA	.35
Snohomish	WASH	.33
Benewah	ID	.32
Bingham	ID	.31
Bannock	ID	.30
Lyman	SD	.29
Fremont	WY	.29
Lake	MONT	.26
Sioux	ND	.24
St.Louis	MINN	.22
Rosebud	MONT	.21
Otero	NM	.19
Harney	OR	.17
Okanogan	WASH	.17
Missoula	MONT	.17
Cattaraugus	NY	.16
Glades	FL	.15
Glacier	MONT	.12
Whatcom	WASH	-.10

Table 4.4 (Continued)

RANK	COUNTY	ST	HOMICIDE RATE	COUNTY	ST	SOCIAL DISORG.	COUNTY	ST	POVERTY INDEX
66	Day	SD	29.52	Pima	AZ	-.04	Apache	AZ	.09
67	Lyman	SD	29.67	Burnett	WIS	-.01	Swain	AZ	.09
68	Brouward	FL	30.01	Douglas	NEV	.00	Lewis	ID	-.08
69	Yakima	WASH	30.61	LaPlata	CO	.01	MCKinley	NM	-.05
70	Benewah	ID	30.72	Idaho	ID	.02	Yakima	WASH	-.02
71	King	WASH	31.14	McLean	ND	.03	Mahnomen	MINN	-.01
72	Valencia	NM	32.89	Beltrami	MN	.04	Valencia	NM	-.01
73	Wood	WIS	32.92	Maricopa	AZ	.14	Jackson	NC	-.00
74	Hendry	FL	33.61	Washington	ME	.15	Blaine	MONT	.00
75	Jefferson	OR	33.90	Lewis	ID	.18	Hill	MONT	.01
76	Burnett	WIS	34.09	NezPerce	ID	.19	Navajo	AZ	.09
77	Inyo	CA	34.26	Todd	SD	.26	Sawyer	WI	.17
78	Sioux	ND	34.80	Bingham	ID	.26	Imperial	CA	.21
79	Uintah	UT	34.95	Benson	ND	.27	Coconino	AZ	.26
80	Leake	MISS	35.54	Yellowstone	MONT	.29	Graham	AZ	.27
81	Yellowstone	MONT	35.82	Washoe	NEV	.32	Montezuma	CO	.29
82	Umatilla	OR	36.89	CarsonCity	NEV	.33	Roosevelt	MONT	.31
83	Koochiching	MINN	38.71	Nye	NEV	.33	CharlesMix	SD	.32
84	Nye	NEV	38.82	Buffalo	SD	.35	Gila	AZ	.33
85	Maricopa	AZ	39.59	Sioux	ND	.36	Dewey	SD	.34
86	Fremont	WY	39.63	Snohomish	WASH	.38	Pierce	WASH	.39
87	Missoula	MONT	39.82	Umatilla	OR	.41	Humboldt	NEV	.43
88	Glacier	MONT	40.17	Ashland	WIS	.42	Newton	MISS	.45
89	Modoc	CA	40.36	DelNorte	CA	.49	Mountrail	ND	.54
90	Sawyer	WI	40.38	Knox	NEB	.52	Riverside	CA	.54
91	Mason	WASH	40.47	Mendocino	CA	.56	SanJuan	UT	.55
92	Fresno	CA	41.04	Yavopai	AZ	.66	Beltrami	MN	.56
93	Shannon	SD	41.28	Mountrail	ND	.68	Yavopai	AZ	.63

94	Yuma	AZ	42.20
95	Pondera	MONT	42.39
96	Glades	FL	42.64
97	Gila	AZ	42.74
98	Blaine	MONT	42.77
99	Buffalo	SD	42.87
100	Wasco	OR	44.71
101	Roberts	SD	44.84
102	Pinal	AZ	45.28
103	Roosevelt	MONT	48.98
104	McLean	ND	49.52
105	Otero	NM	50.39
106	Imperial	CA	50.41
107	Swain	NC	54.80
108	Newton	MISS	54.95
109	Kootnai	ID	59.15
110	Knox	NEB	60.28
111	Todd	SD	61.98
112	Polk	WIS	63.21
113	Lewis	ID	64.94
114	Rosebud	MONT	71.93
115	Corson	SD	72.18
116	Sauk	WIS	73.26
117	Marshall	SD	97.51
118	Douglas	NEV	103.52
119	Harney	OR	127.55
120	Idaho	ID	140.06

Riverside	CA	.73		Pima	AZ	.75
Okanogan	WASH	.73		King	WASH	.81
Benewah	ID	.73		Benson	ND	.82
Corson	SD	.83		Tulare	CA	.83
Skagit	WASH	.84		Todd	SD	.86
Harney	OR	.90		Clark	NEV	.91
Tulare	CA	.98		Becker	MINN	.92
Sawyer	WI	1.01		Yuma	AZ	.92
Newton	MISS	1.04		Skagit	WASH	.97
Day	SD	1.08		Washington	ME	.97
Fresno	CA	1.09		Mendocino	CA	1.00
Clark	NEV	1.11		Roberts	SD	1.01
Lyman	SD	1.12		Pinal	AZ	1.10
Roberts	SD	1.12		Fresno	CA	1.13
Brown	KS	1.30		Buffalo	SD	1.13
Imperial	CA	1.35		Rolette	ND	1.15
CharlesMix	SD	1.39		Marshall	SD	1.18
Kootnai	ID	1.47		Shannon	SD	1.26
Thurston	NEB	1.55		Corson	SD	1.49
Modoc	CA	1.66		Hendry	FL	1.51
Humboldt	CA	1.92		Koochiching	MINN	1.57
Inyo	CA	1.97		Maricopa	AZ	1.60
Humboldt	NEV	2.00		Pondera	MONT	1.84
St.Louis	MINN	2.01		Modoc	CA	1.93
Brouward	FL	2.35		Mason	WASH	2.05
Pierce	WASH	2.89		Sauk	WIS	2.83
Wood	WIS	3.46		Polk	WIS	4.10

Note: . Denotes data are missing for this county.

defined poverty level, (2) the percentage of American Indians unemployed, and (3) the percentage of American Indians aged sixteen to
nineteen who are not enrolled in school and who are not high school
graduates (i.e., the dropout rate). The eighth column in Table 4.4 lists the
counties in rank order based on this index.

Each of these indicators is believed to measure different spheres of
economic deprivation. The number of families below the poverty level
has been identified by other investigators as a contributor to high levels
of homicide, as has the unemployment rate.[5] Although there is little
direct evidence of a relationship between the high school dropout rate
and homicide, Loftin and Hill (1974) include it in their "Structural
Poverty Index," which did prove significant when explaining variation
in homicide rates.

Controls. The percentage of the American Indian population that is
aged eighteen to twenty-four and the percentage of the population that is
American Indian were included in the analysis as demographic controls.

Homicide Rates

The homicide rates used in this analysis are presented in the fourth
column of Table 4.4. The incidents of homicide used to calculate these
rates cover the entire 1980-1987 period, not individual years. Because we
are now dealing with very small units (counties), all of the years for
which homicide data were available were used. As with the state-level
analysis, this procedure was used to reduce the influence of random
aberrations in year-to-year estimates, in addition to controlling for the
unreliability of rates based on low frequencies. The total American
Indian homicide rate at the county level was calculated by employing
both denominators and numerators obtained from the Indian Health
Service. The formula for rate calculation was as follows:

$$[(I/P \times 100,000]/8$$

where I = the total number of incidents of American Indian murder in
that county and P = the total American Indian population of that county.
The division by eight indicates that the rates are calculated over the
1980-1987 period and then expressed on a per-year basis. These rates
were also logarithmically transformed to base 10 (see the previous section for a detailed rationale for the transformations).

Table 4.5 displays the zero-order correlations of all variables included
in the indexes with the total American Indian homicide rate. At this
level, only the percentage of high school dropouts retains a significant
relationship with homicide.

Table 4.6 presents the results of a regression analysis of American
Indian homicide. This model results in an R-square of .41. Both the social

Table 4.5
**Correlation Matrix of the Total American Indian Homicide Rate
and All American Indian–Specific Variables Included in the Indexes
(*N* = 114 Reservation Counties)**

		1	2	3	4	5	6	7	8
1.	Homicide	–							
2.	%Movers	.08	–						
3.	%Female House	.16	.16	–					
4.	%Poor	.18	-.18	.13	–				
5.	%Unemployed	.14	-.03	.05	.01	–			
6.	%Dropouts	.31*	-.03	.12	.36**	.19	–		
7.	%18-24	-.18	-.03	.03	.05	-.13	.17	–	
8.	%Amer.Ind.	.07	-.39**	.09	.38	.04	.02	.05	–

Note: %Female House = Percent of American Indian families who are female headed with no husband and children under the age of 18; %Movers = Percent of American Indians who did not live on this reservation in 1979 or 1980; %Poor = Percent of American Indian families below the Poverty Level; %Unemployed = Percent of American Indians unemployed; %Dropouts = Percent of American Indians aged 16-19 who are not enrolled in school and who are not high school graduates; %18-24 = Percent of the American Indian population that is aged 18-24; %Amer. Ind. = Percent of the population that is American Indian.

disorganization and poverty indexes are significant predictors of American Indian homicide at the reservation county level. The demographic controls of percentage of American Indian population aged eighteen to twenty-four and percentage of the population that is American Indian are not significantly related to Indian homicide. This might possibly be because there is relatively little variation in these variables at the reservation county level.

Thus, for reservation communities, support is provided for both hypotheses. High levels of social disorganization are significantly related to high levels of homicide in reservation communities, as are high levels of economic deprivation. As both instability and poverty increase within these communities, so do levels of lethal violence.

SUMMARY

This chapter has presented multivariate analyses of American Indian homicide at the state and reservation county levels. While only our second hypothesis was supported at the state level, both hypotheses

Table 4.6
**Regression Analysis of the American Indian Homicide Rate for
Four American Indian–Specific Independent Variables, 1980-1987
(*N* = 114 Reservation Counties)**

	B	SE B	Beta	t
Social Disorganization	.04	.02	.16	2.28*
Poverty	.08	.02	.31	3.44*
Pct Amer. Ind.	.02	.04	.04	.51
Pct Aged 18-24	-.01	.05	-.20	-1.81

Note: Social Disorganization = Percent of American Indian families who are female headed with no husband and children under the age of 18 plus the percent of American Indians who did not live on this reservation in 1979; Poverty = Percent of American Indian families below the poverty level plus the percent of American Indians unemployed plus the percent of American Indians aged 16-19 who are not enrolled in school and who are not high school graduates; Pct Amer. Ind. = Percent of the population that is American Indian; Pct Aged 18-24 = Percent of the American Indian population that is aged 18-24.

* = 1-tailed significance: p = .01.

were supported when reservation counties were employed as the unit of analysis. Regression results indicate that both social disorganization and economic deprivation contribute to high levels of lethal violence in reservation communities.

While this research has only tested two elements of the model proposed in Chapter 3, it has added a great deal of insight into what is known about the etiology of American Indian homicide at the aggregate level.

Future research must investigate other possible sources of lethal violence among the American Indian population, such as culture conflict, a subculture of violence, and alcoholism. To enable this investigation at an aggregate level, attention must focus on developing measures for these variables. Other variables, such as medical resource availability and discriminatory imposition of the law, may also contribute to high levels of lethal violence among American Indians and must also be explored in future empirical work. Chapter 5 will provide a discussion of these alternative explanations of American Indian homicide.

NOTES

1. Thomas & Znaniecki, 1920; Park & Burgess, 1921; Shaw & McKay, 1969.
2. See Loftin & Hill, 1974; Williams, 1984; Loftin & Parker, 1985; and Williams & Flewelling, 1988.

3. With this exclusion of states not containing reservations, the model estimated may contain sample selection bias. "By excluding some observations in a systematic manner, one has inadvertently introduced the need for an additional regressor that the usual least squares procedures ignore: in effect, one has produced the traditional specification error that results when an omitted regressor is correlated with an included regressor" (Berk, 1983, p. 388). Anytime potential observations from some population of interest (in this case, states) are excluded from a sample on a nonrandom basis, one risks sample selection bias. In this analysis, steps offered by Berk (1983) were followed to correct for the explicit selection of reservation states, while excluding nonreservation states. These steps are as follows:

(1) A probit or logit model of the selection process is estimated with the dummy endogenous variable coded "0" when the observation on the substantive endogenous variable is missing [nonreservation state] and "1" when it was present [reservation state].

(2) The predicted values from the probit equation are saved. These predicted values represent a random, normal variable.

(3) From the predicated values, the hazard rate is constructed. [In this research, the hazard rate is simply the predicted values.]

(4) The hazard rate is then treated as a new variable and included in any substantive equations [any equations predicting American Indian homicide using only reservation states as the units of analysis]. (Berk, 1983, p. 393)

Although it is safe to assume that the sample selection bias will be small, particularly since this research entails explicit selection compared to a survey framework, as Berk (1983) concludes, "Perhaps the best advice is always to begin with the assumption that sample selection bias exists and proceed where possible with the corrections unless a strong argument can be made that moots the problem" (p. 396). Accordingly, corrected estimated equations were performed at the state level. However, results obtained from the corrected models were no different from those obtained from the uncorrected models. Consequently, the uncorrected models are presented in this chapter to prevent unnecessary confusion.

4. Crutchfield, Geerken, & Gove, 1982; Williams & Flewelling, 1988; Baron & Straus, 1989; Browne & Williams, 1989.

5. Williams, 1984; Williams & Flewelling, 1988; Bachman, Linsky, & Straus, 1988.

Chapter 5

Alternative Explanations of American Indian Homicide

In the last two chapters, we have explored the etiology of American Indian homicide at both individual and aggregate levels. We have found that many factors contribute to lethal violence within this population, including economic deprivation, social disorganization, a subculture of violence, culture conflict and perceived powerlessness, and alcohol abuse. It was also noted that the process of internal colonialism was antecedent to these and was perhaps the catalyst that caused these other deleterious conditions to develop. However, alternative explanations can be offered when explaining the high rates of homicide that exist for American Indians. The purpose of this chapter is to provide the reader with discussions of two of these alternatives: (1) the discriminatory imposition of the law that may exist against American Indians and (2) a lack of medical resources in many American Indian communities.

RACIAL CHARACTERISTICS AND THE IMPOSITION OF THE LAW

A proliferation of theoretical writing holds that the impositon of the law in our country is a selective process that operates to the disadvantage of poor and minority defendants (Quinney, 1979; Chambliss and Seidman, 1971). One of the most frequently cited of the studies that document this argument is that of Chambliss and Seidman (1971). Operating from a conflict perspective, these authors formulate a theory of the legal process that they believe operates in most complex societies, including our own. Included in the propositions of their theory are the following:

The legal system is organized through bureaucratically structured agencies . . . the rules [of this system] are for a variety of reasons frequently vague, ambiguous, contradictory, or weakly or inadequately sanctioned. Therefore, each level of the bureaucracy possesses considerable discretion as to the performance of its duties. In complex societies, political power is closely tied to social position. Therefore, those laws which prohibit certain types of behavior popular among lower-class persons are more likely to be enforced, while laws restricting the behavior of middle or upper-class persons are not likely to be enforced. Where laws are so stated that people of all classes are equally likely to violate them, the lower the social position of an offender, the greater is the likelihood that sanctions will be imposed on him. When sanctions are imposed, the most severe sanctions will be imposed on persons in the lowest social class. (pp. 474-475)

Along with Chambliss and Seidman, others argue that the inequalities that exist in our legal system result not only from direct discrimination against poor or minority groups, but also from these groups' lack of access to the resources required to prepare a successful defense.

Black (1976) has more specifically delineated the quantity and style of law that operates in almost every setting. According to his theory, Black argues, stratification is the vertical aspect under which social life operates. In *The Behavior of Law*, he states, "It [stratification] is any uneven distribution of the material conditions of existence, such as food and shelter, and the means by which these are produced, such as land, raw materials, tools, domestic animals, and slaves. . . . In a broad sense, then, stratification is inequality of wealth" (p. 11). Black goes on to explain that when wealth is unevenly distributed among the people (i.e., when stratification exists), then each person is higher or lower in relation to others. Thus, each person has a rank or vertical status. Law, Black believes, varies directly with this rank or status. He postulates several relationships that exist between the law and this status, including the following:

An upward crime [one committed by a lower-ranked person against a higher-ranked person] is more likely to receive a serious charge. . . . The wealthier a thief is, for instance, the less serious is his theft. Thus, in modern America, department stores are less likely to prosecute shoplifters who are middle-class and white than those who are lower-class and black, and in court, the same applies to the likelihood of conviction, a jail sentence, and a sentence of 30 days or more. . . . It is possible to order the seriousness of deviant behavior according to its vertical location and direction, at once. All else constant, upward deviance is the most serious, followed by deviant behavior between people of high rank, then between people of low rank and finally downward deviance. The quantity of law decreases accordingly, and this applies to law of every kind. In cases of homicide, for example, the most severe punishment befalls a poor man who kills a wealthy man, followed by a wealthy man who kills another equally wealthy, then a poor man whose victim is equally poor, while the least severe punishment is given to a wealthy man who kills a poor man. (p. 24)

While Black's theories are directed at the process by which our legal system deals with crime and deviance in general, other writers have more specifically criticized the comparative homicide literature for not taking this potential discrimination into account when developing theories of homicide causation. The most impassioned critique of this kind comes from Hawkins (1986), who charges that most investigators of homicide completely ignore how the judicial system of this country regulates criminal behavior.

Espousing a theory similar to Black's vertical theory of law, Hawkins (1986) believes that the historical behavior of American law, particularly during the slavery era, created a hierarchy of seriousness in relation to criminal violence that was based primarily on the racial identity of the offender and the relationship that existed between the victim and the offender. In this hierarchy, the killing of a White person in authority by a Black person is seen as the most serious offense, whereas the killing of a Black inmate by a White person is the least serious. Hawkins states that "blacks may have come to believe that aggressive behavior of all types directed by blacks against each other will be tolerated and seldom severely punished." He determines that Black life is seen as cheap in our society, and White life is valuable.

This hypothesis could easily be extended to the American Indian population. The disregard for Black life during the slavery era was no more brutal than that experienced by the Indians during the westward expansion. This is certainly validated by the virtual extinction of the entire American Indian people. Further, evidence abounds that these degrading attitudes and disregard for American Indian life are alive and well among the general population today, particularly non-Indians who live on or near reservations. For example, during a field study on three mid-western reservations, I was told on more than a few occasions, "Well, you know, the only good Indian is a dead Indian." (See Chapter 8 for a more detailed account of this devaluation of Indian life.)

Because research on racial disparities in legal decisions has remained equivocal (see Kleck, 1981), some have argued that discrimination in the legal process may be operating more subtly through institutionalized stereotypes of criminality, rather than through overt behavior. Schur's (1971) words describing the relationship that exists between stereotypes and deviance are pertinent here:

Stereotyping, then, both in general and as a feature of deviance and control situations has dual significance. On one hand, it reflects the needs of participants in complex interactions to order their expectations so that they can predict the actions of others, at least to an extent sufficient for coherent organization of their own behavior. On the other hand, when we think of the selective perception frequently involved in this process, we recognize that the potential for reactions based on inaccurate assessments is substantial. (p. 41)

Swigert and Farrell (1977) were perhaps the first to apply this line of reasoning to the study of decision-making practices in the legal process. These authors speculate that, more than class and race, cultural stereotypes of criminality determine the decisions of legal authorities. After reviewing the psychiatric portions of evaluations obtained from a clinic attached to a court in a large urban jurisdiction, these authors report the surfacing of a diagnostic category that seemed to reflect official usage of what Swigert and Farrell term a "normal primitive" stereotype. The clinical description of this diagnosis stated that the spontaneous expressions of violence that characterize this stereotype are almost endemic to certain poor and minority populations. In summary, this "normal primitive" was characterized as being

comfortable and without mental illness. He has little, if any education and is of dull intelligence. His goals are sensual and immediate—satisfying his physical and sexual needs without inhibition, postponement or planning. There is little regard for the future—extending hardly beyond the filling of his stomach and the net pay or relief check. His loyalties and identification are with a group that has little purpose in life, except surviving with a minimum of sweat and a maximum of pleasure. (p. 19)

This imagery suggests that one who is unfortunate enough to be labeled in this way is stereotyped as having a predisposition to violence that culminates both from that individual's life style and from his or her innate attributes. Swigert and Farrell (1977) found that this stereotype was more often applied to Black and lower-class defendants who were less likely to obtain bail or a jury trial and who, consequently, received more severe sentences.

This stereotypical definition bears close resemblance to one of the most pervasive stereotypes that exists about the American Indian people. Stereotypes like the "normal primitive" uncovered by Swigert and Farrell (1977) are revealed in the imagery of the "noble savage" in relation to American Indian populations. One of the earliest writings to reflect this stereotype is a letter written by a missionary in this country in 1628:

As to the natives of this country, I find them entirely savage and wild, strangers to all decency, yea, uncivil and stupid as garden stakes, proficient in all wickedness and ungodliness, devilish men who serve nobody but the devil, that is, the spirit which in their language they call Menetto, under which title they comprehend everything that is

subtle and crafty and beyond human skill and power. They are as
thievish and treacherous as they are tall, and in cruelty they are altogether inhuman, more than barbarous, far exceeding the Africans.
(*Annals of America*, 1985, vol. 1, p. 93)

These words reveal the stereotypical image of the "noble savage"
quite clearly. Unfortunately, this stereotype appears to have persisted
ever since its inception with the first European contact with the natives
of this country. For example, after performing a historical analysis of
stereotypes held about the American Indian, Berkhofer (1978) concludes
that many perceptions about American Indian peoples have remained
consistent through time. These include the perception that American
Indians are alternatively noble or ignoble, but nevertheless deficient in
intellect, accomplishment, and culture. Other research, which has investigated such things as educational materials and popular media, has concluded that American Indians continue to be labeled in inaccurate, static,
and derogatory terms.[1] Although positive images of American Indian
peoples, such as those depicted in the movie *Dances with Wolves*, have
appeared recently, negative stereotypes continue to pervade popular
literature and media representations, and, most importantly, to persist in
people's minds. How pervasive are such stereotypes of American
Indians in the criminal justice system today? What effect do these institutionalized stereotypes have in the legal decision-making process? Although
there have been no attempts to answer these questions directly, empirical
evidence does exist concerning the discriminatory practices of some law
enforcement agencies against the American Indian population.

Pioneering in this literature is a study conducted by Hall and Simkus
(1975). These authors compare sentencing decisions for 1,574 White
offenders and 221 American Indian offenders in a western state. After
controlling for several important factors, including the type of offense,
number of prior felonies, prior juvenile offenses, juvenile institutional-
ization, education level, employment, occupation, marital status, age,
dependents, and average degree of harshness of the sentencing judge,
Hall and Simkus still found significant differences in the sentences
received by American Indian and White offenders.

Assuming that types of sentences may be interpreted from the standpoint of labeling theory, Hall and Simkus (1975) believe that the differences in the type of sentence imposed between Indians and Whites may
represent differences in the application of a criminal label. For example,
a deferred sentence would not be as likely to denote this criminal label,
whereas other sentences do involve applying the label "convicted felon"
to an individual. With this in mind, Hall and Simkus found that the probability of receiving a "convicted felon" label was at least 8 percent
greater for an American Indian offender than for a similar White of-

fender. Further, more than 79 percent of American Indian offenders served time in prison compared to only 63 percent of comparable White offenders. These authors conclude:

From the viewpoint of the native American offender, the inequalities in sentencing reported here are substantial. . . . The native American's relative lack of power and influence, his subjection to the remaining influence of old negative stereotypes as a "drunken, brawling, [horse] stealing Indian," his increased "visibility" outside of the reservation boundaries, and his position in social and economic conflict with the white community may constitute a handicap in his ability to avoid being labeled and incarcerated. His inability to hire effective lawyers, to meet bail demands, and to engage effectively in plea negotiations may further reduce his chances to avoid the more severe types of sentences. (pp. 215-216)

Other empirical evidence of discrimination is offered by Williams (1979). After performing a longitudinal analysis of arrest and disposition rates for all individuals processed by the Seattle Police Department, he concludes that neither low socioeconomic class nor minority status is a sufficient explanation for the significant differentials noted between Whites and American Indians. "Rather, it seems that the urban Indian is in a class all his own, and it is a very unique and negative one" (p. 7). Williams further states:

A potentially valid explanation for the alarming arrest rates for Indians may be as basic as anti-Indian bias on the part of the criminal justice system. Whether correctly or incorrectly, the contemporary Indian often feels that he is the recipient of prejudice and discrimination that other minorities—particularly blacks—have somehow managed to escape. And it is this very climate which can so easily foster an insidious brand of resentment, humiliation, frustration, and anger which may manifest itself in high rates of social deviance." (p. 23)

Many of the offenders I interviewed expressed feelings consistent with Williams' contention. For example, respondent thirteen explains:

Even my lawyer told me that I wouldn't be in this prison if I had $10,000. All the evidence was there, but I had a public defender with no brains. If you have money you're O.K., but if you don't—good-bye—we will see you in fucking 10 years. That's just the way it is. That's the system. They fabricate evidence, lie and everything. Then they say plead guilty and we'll go easy on you. You don't have any rights—you just do exactly what they tell you to do.

Many other offenders talked about the experience of being labeled and feeling unable to break the cycle. One stated, "Even when you try to change—people won't let you. It's like you fucked up, now you're fucked up so fuck off! It's like a fox who can't get out and is just waiting for someone to come and shoot him."

A significant proportion of the men I interviewed believed that they had experienced discriminatory practices by the criminal justice system. Some even recalled incidents that had happened to them at an early age. For example:

> My first experience with the law was when I was thirteen, and a white kid and I hid some marijuana under a trailer house. Some lady seen us and told the police that some Indian had hid something under there, and sure enough, I was the one who got in trouble and sent to reform school. That white kid is probably still breaking the law, but who is in jail now? Even if he did kill someone, he would have a better chance of beating it than me or any other Indian. (respondent 12)

Many spoke about the unfair circumstances surrounding their trials. Although this may not be an uncommon perception among convicted homicide offenders, regardless of race, some accounts described to me are too revealing to go unmentioned. For example, one respondent described this:

> When the cops came in after the fight, I had cuts and bruises all over my body—I still have scars [he points to a few]. I was all swollen and stuff with blood everywhere. I was bleeding from cuts from *his* knife. The cops came in and took pictures of me to show this to the jury—I thought—because it was self-defense. I killed him in self-defense obviously. Well, at the trial, they said that they didn't have film in the camera. Can you believe that? No film in the camera when they took pictures of me, yet they took over 52 pictures of him during the autopsy and everything. And they showed every damn one of them in the trial. You know, I just had a public defender and he didn't do anything about it. You know how pictures are to a jury. There were a lot of things that went on during the trial that just weren't right, but nothing that I could do. I was just a stupid kid with a stupid public defender—no rights. I just did what they told me to do. Plead guilty, they said, or you'll get sent to prison for longer. What a system! (respondent 9)

Another respondent states:

> You know I was tried by an all-white jury. The law states that you are supposed to be tried by your peers, but there were no Indians on that jury. There were two of them for jury duty, but they were dismissed from my trial. I ended up with turkey farmers and shit—people like that—all white. Most didn't even pay attention to what was going on, especially when my side was heard. When I was on the stand, one

guy sitting in the back of the jury couldn't hear. He kept hollering in the courtroom—"Hey, I can't hear what's going on back here"—and shit like that. The trial was right off the reservation so you know these people were a little if not a lot prejudiced. One guy on the jury just kept glaring at me the whole time. I got handed down the max, and everyone else who was up—you know my friend—they postponed their trials until they got a different jury in there. That should tell you something. (respondent 21)

Besides describing discriminatory practices they experienced during impositions and trials, some offenders also talked about being physically and emotionally abused by the police. Two interview narratives illustrate these perceptions quite clearly:

I learned my lesson with the police. They beat me, shot at me, dislocated my elbow, put my face through doors and glass and cut me up. [He points to a scar that runs from his forehead across his eye to his cheek.] Made me feel like I was just a piece of shit. (respondent 14)

They would always come into the bars and stuff—you know there would be white guys in there, too, but we were always the ones that got carted off to jail. They would always slap me around and shit before they put me in the cell. I seen this happen all the time, too. And if a white guy ever had a little too much to drink, he always got taken home and tucked into bed like a nice little boy. (respondent 29)

It seems apparent that at least some degree of discriminatory behavior on the part of the criminal justice system against American Indians does exist in this country. However, it is important to reiterate that there are very few studies that specifically investigate sentence disparities between American Indians and Whites. Further, the literature, which has primarily focused on Black and White differentials, remains equivocal. The literature addressing this question is extensive, and it is beyond the scope of this chapter to review it in its entirety. The primary purpose of this section is to bring these issues to the reader's attention. Even though I was not able to empirically assess the degree to which discrimination played a role in the arrest and conviction of both the American Indian offenders interviewed here and those represented by the aggregate-level homicide data, the discriminatory imposition of the law must certainly be noted when studying homicide causation, particularly among minority groups in our country.

Another factor that may contribute to high rates of lethal violence among American Indian populations is differential access to medical resources. This issue will be highlighted next.

MEDICAL RESOURCES: AN EPIDEMIOLOGICAL
PROFILE OF HOMICIDE

Suppose that you are a White male who lives in a large metropolitan area. One night, while you and your friends are partying at one of the local night spots, another intoxicated man comes up to you and starts abusing you with verbal jeers like "Hey, you scum, you candy ass!" This eventually escalates until you are both out in the parking lot of the bar in a physical fight. Before anyone can stop him, the other man pulls a knife and stabs you in the side. Your friends immediately call an ambulance, which arrives within fifteen minutes, and you are whisked away to an area hospital. Here you are treated for your wounds and recover within a few days.

Now imagine that you are an American Indian male who lives on a small reservation located in a very remote setting. One night, while you are out drinking with your friends, a fight ensues between you and another Indian male. He pulls out a knife, and you are soon lying on the ground in a pool of blood. There is no ambulance in the community for your friends to call. They drag your body into their car and start driving you to the nearest hospital, which is located about fifty miles away. The roads, however, are gravel, and they can only travel about forty miles an hour. When you arrive, you are unconscious and have lost so much blood that the medical technicians are unable to save your life.

These different scenarios elucidate the vast differences that can exist in medical resource availability. They also illustrate quite clearly that the extent to which an individual has access to medical resources often makes the difference between life and death. In the medical literature, all forms of homicide are classified as injuries (Baker, 1985). A case of homicide is operationally defined as being caused by acute exposure to physical agents, such as mechanical energy, interacting with the body in amounts and at rates that exceed the threshold of human tolerance. Although differential access to medical care by race/ethnicity has not been empirically documented, some authors speculate on its existence.[2]

Two of the most ambitious studies to date are those of Doerner (1983, Doerner & Speir, 1986). Doerner suggests that medical care is the "missing link" that determines whether interpersonal violence escalates from a case of aggravated assault to a case of homicide. Medical resource availability could therefore become an intervening component in the production of homicide rates not only by region, but also by race. Although Doerner's analysis of certain medical variables (e.g., number of doctors and nurses in a given area) did not provide unequivocal evidence that medical care does provide this missing link, it did explain part of the variance in homicide differentials.

In another study, Williams and Bachman (1988) analyzed weapon-specific rates of homicide. These authors used a medical resource availability index composed of several indicators, including numbers of doctors, nurses, emergency rooms, and hospital beds. They found that this medical resource availability index was a significant and negative predictor of homicides that involved the use of knives only. That is, states with a greater number of medical resources had significantly fewer knife homicide deaths compared to states with fewer medical resources. These results did not hold for deaths caused by other weapons, such as those resulting from guns. This is a logical finding because assaults with guns often result in instantaneous death, whereas death from a knife wound is more often a slow process of bleeding to death. Therefore, homicides involving knives would have a greater chance of being prevented by the availability of fast and accessible medical resources.

This is an important finding, particularly regarding the American Indian population. If you will remember from Chapter 2, American Indian homicides are proportionately more likely to involve knives than any other weapon. For this reason, medical resource availability could be a very important variable to control for when attempting to explain American Indian homicide rates.

SUMMARY

This chapter has considered two alternative explanations of American Indian homicide that were not accounted for in earlier chapters. Qualitative information provided by homicide offenders interviewed for this research, as well as empirical evidence offered by other investigators, indicates that American Indian offenders may be the victims of discriminatory practices by our judicial system. This discrimination may be manifested in many ways; for example, Indians having a higher probability of being apprehended for a crime, being convicted of a crime, and receiving a harsher sentence for a crime. Further, key players in our judicial system may hold negative stereotypes of the American Indian population, which may be the impetus for each of these discriminatory practices.

Another variable considered was medical resource availability. American Indian homicide rate differentials may be greatly affected by the extent to which those in the population have access to immediate and adequate medical care. Given the fact that approximately one-half of the Indian population resides on relatively isolated reservations, an American Indian who is wounded in the course of a conflict situation may have a decreased chance of receiving adequate medical attention and, consequently, may die. This structural circumstance may more often escalate acts of assault to homicide in the American Indian population compared to the population in general.

Future research must provide a closer examination of how the issues of medical resource availability and discriminatory imposition of the law affect the rate of homicide in the American Indian population. More research is clearly needed that qualitatively investigates the stereotypical perceptions that some in our judicial system may hold for American Indian people and how these perceptions influence the processing of an Indian offender.

With regard to medical resource availability, research can take many avenues. For example, one question that arises from this discussion is, Do reservation communities that have more medical services per capita have lower fatality rates from assaults? Further, what is the average length of time needed for a victim of assault to receive medical attention in reservation communities compared to urban centers? Each of these areas of inquiry is essential in order to complete the picture of American Indian homicide that has been sketched in this book.

The next chapter will move on to investigate another form of aggression that is directed outward toward others: violence in American Indian families.

NOTES

1. Using a more educated college sample, Hanson and Rouse (1987, 1900) found that fewer negative stereotypes existed, particularly when students were given accurate information about the American Indian people.

2. Gastil, 1971; Loftin and Hill, 1974; Murphy, 1974.

Chapter 6

Violence in American Indian Families

> We try to deal with one problem here because you can't fix them all. Here we try to put back together lives that have been destroyed because of family violence. You know you have so many problems here that it is overwhelming. I believe almost everyone on the reservation is affected by alcoholism either directly or indirectly. If you are talking about actual addiction to alcohol—maybe 70 percent are addicted. And unemployment is a comparable percentage (around 80%). As a result, there is a lot of violence here and a lot of it is directed inside the family structure itself. And in many cases we are not just talking about slaps; we are talking about severe violence, knifings, and shootings.

The above statement was made by the director of a battered women's shelter located on a midwestern reservation. The shelter has been in operation since 1987 and has nearly quadrupled in size since that time. As one counselor states, "We keep building additions and there never seems to be enough room. It is terrible when you have to turn someone away. We have people who offer their homes in cases of emergency— homes that we will use when we have to—but it is just a bad situation."

While most in our society would view the family as a place where love and affection abound, some researchers have found that it is often the place where violence is most likely to occur. In fact Straus, Gelles, and Steinmetz (1980) conclude that "the family is the most physically violent group or institution that a typical citizen is likely to encounter" (p. 13).

Despite the proliferation of studies on family violence in this country, little attention has been focused on minority groups, including American

Indians. While some investigators have studied child maltreatment in American Indian communities (Fischler, 1985), virtually none has focused attention on issues of spousal violence. The paucity of research on family violence among American Indians parallels the paucity of services. In fact, while the population in general has had access to battered women's shelters for nearly two decades (albeit limited in some communities), the few shelters that do exist for American Indian women on reservations were only opened within the last few years.

The purpose of this chapter is to examine some epidemiological findings regarding issues of violence among American Indian families. The first section of this chapter will present findings from my fieldwork at three battered women's shelters located on reservations. The second section will present national estimates of the incidence of violence among American Indian families from the 1985 National Family Violence Resurvey (Straus & Gelles, 1990). Using 204 families who identified themselves as American Indian, incidence rates of both couple violence in general and husband-to-wife violence will be presented. Finally, using this same data set, the etiology of this violence will be explored. Statistical tests will be conducted that examine the extent to which violence in American Indian families can be explained by alcohol abuse and stress, taking into account other demographic characteristics of American Indian families that may also explain the violence occurring within them.

Before beginning, however, it is important to define exactly what is meant by "domestic violence." For purposes of this chapter, the definition of domestic violence used is that proposed by Straus and Gelles (1989). They define violence as "an act carried out with the intention or perceived intention of physically hurting another person" (p. 20). This "hurt" can range from the pain caused by a slap to the severe injury or even death caused by more violent acts.

Note that the key elements in this definition are "act" and "intention." Whether or not the act results in injury or not is not important here; rather, what is important is the act itself. What must be examined is whether the intent was to cause pain, in which case an act may or may not be considered violence. If a husband attempts to shoot his wife and misses, it is still considered violence. Similarly, if a woman is accidently hit in the head with a ball during a racquetball game, this would not be defined as violence because there was no intent to cause injury.

For the present purposes, this chapter will focus primarily on physical violence. This does not imply that physical acts are the only types of abuse that family members can inflict on each other. Verbal aggression and sexual assault among family members can certainly be harmful. However, a detailed discussion of these forms of maltreatment is beyond the scope of this chapter.

THE REALITY OF VIOLENCE IN
AMERICAN INDIAN FAMILIES

The information in this section comes from interviews and data that were collected at three battered women's shelters located on two midwestern reservations and one northeastern reservation. The interviews were conducted by this author and the data were collected in the summers of 1987 and 1989. A total of twelve American Indian women who were residing at the shelters, were interviewed, as were fourteen social workers and counselors who worked at the shelters. The interviews were unstructured in nature and lasted from one to three hours. Because the sample size is too small for generalizations to be made, the information and case studies presented in this section are for illustration purposes only.

Each of the shelters was relatively new and had been in operation for an average of two years. Two shelters, however, had developed a structured intake questionnaire, which was administered to all women requesting assistance. Table 6.1 presents responses from these intake questionnaires. It can be seen, from this table, that the majority of the women who sought help at these shelters were abused by their husbands (52 percent) compared to those abused by either their boyfriends (27 percent) or someone else (21 percent). In a vast majority of these cases, the abuser was under the influence of drugs or alcohol when committing the assault (75 percent), while only 19 percent of the victims were under the influence. It can also be seen that in 35 percent of the cases, physical injuries were sustained, and 11 percent of those physically injured were treated by a physician. Of the women who filled out these intake questionnaires, 77 percent reported that this was not the first incident, and 62 percent of them were willing to sign a restraining order. When asked about the length of time that the abuse had been occurring, the highest percentge of cases (36 percent) reported that the abuse had been happening within the last eleven months.

Before we move on, I want to provide the reader with a few case studies. These perhaps typify the circumstances that surrounded most of the abuse cases I encountered. To facilitate presentation and to protect the anonymity of these women, I will use the pseudonyms Debbie and Joan for the women in the case studies presented below.

Debbie

Debbie was born on a small midwestern reservation in the early 1960s. Every relationship she has had with a man has been abusive, beginning with her father. Her first marriage began without incidence of violence, but this soon changed. She states, "He would be so nice and caring, but

Table 6.1
**Percentage of Responses to Intake Questionnaires at
Two Battered Women's Shelters (N = 92)**

Question and Responses	Percentages
Who is the Abuser?	
Husband	52%
Boyfriend	27%
Other	21%
Was the Abuser under the influence of alcohol or drugs?	
Yes	75%
No	25%
Were you under the influence of alcohol or drugs?	
Yes	19%
No	77%
No Response	4%
Are there physical injuries?	
Yes	35%
No	65%
Have the injuries been treated by an MD/PA?	
Yes	11%
No	89%
Was this the first incident?	
Yes	21%
No	77%
No Response	1%
How long has the abuse been happening?	
0-11 months	36%
1 to 2 years	13%
2 to 6 years	25%
7 to 10 years	16%
More than 10 years	10%
Are you willing to sign a restraining order?	
Yes	62%
No	30%
No Response	8%

as soon as the relationship got old, it just turned out violent." Most incidents occurred in the context of a jealous rage during a drinking binge.

The assault that brought Debbie to the shelter occurred in the spring of 1987. Debbie was eight months pregnant and home with her son one Saturday night, while her husband was out with his friends. Her husband returned to the house drunk, screaming and yelling accusations that she was fooling around with other men. "He was yelling crazy things like I had been with other men and that the baby I was carrying probably wasn't even his." He padlocked the front door from the outside so

Debbie could not leave the house. He also locked their son in a storage closet so that he could not see what was happening or run for help.

He started by pouring Pine-sol, ketchup, syrup, and "anything he could grab" on her head, and then he made her go and take a shower. When she was clean, he would do the same thing again. During this time, he continued to drink.

This continued throughout the night. In the morning, he let their son out of the closet and sent him to school, while he had Debbie locked in their bedroom. When their son was gone, the physical abuse began. Debbie states, "He had my curling iron and a curtain rod in his hands and was hitting me with them. I was just laying on the bed. I couldn't do anything. He kicked me, too, all over." Several hours later, a friend came and knocked on the door. While her husband went to answer it, Debbie escaped out the bedroom window, ran to the nearest house for help, and was taken to the hospital. She sustained many injuries, including large bruises and welts across her back, cigarette burns on her right foot, a black eye, and two large patches of hair missing, and she needed seven stitches on the right side of her head. Debbie also started having contractions, which were diagnosed as stress-related and subsided shortly.

Debbie placed a restraining order on her husband. He was picked up by tribal police the following night. However, he was released from jail within twenty-four hours. When Debbie was escorted by a tribal police officer to her home to pick up her belongings, they found her and her son's clothes, mostly burned, thrown all over the yard. This case is still pending in tribal court.

Joan

Joan has spent most of her twenty-six years of life on a reservation. She had a relatively trouble-free life compared to her friends; both of her parents had stopped drinking when she was very young, and she felt "secure and safe with her family" when she was young.

When she entered junior high school, her world changed rapidly. She felt pressure from her friends to start drinking. Getting drunk every weekend became the norm, as did drinking binges once or twice during the week. When she was sixteen, she was going steady with a man who was four years older than she. They did everything together, including drink. Although the beginning of the relationship was not characterized by violence, drunken escapades soon led to physical assaults by her boyfriend. "He would usually get drunk and accuse me of things—get jealous—mostly for things that he would imagine. Sometimes I wouldn't even be with him, and he would come looking for me all mad. When he sobered up, he would be sorry and crying and everything, and I would always forgive him."

Joan became pregnant when she was seventeen. Although she chose to remain unmarried, both she and her boyfriend played a role in bringing up their child. The arrival of their daughter, however, did not stop the drinking and violence. The drinking remained constant, and the violence seemed to escalate. "It got to where he didn't even have to be drunk to hit me."

This was Joan's life for five years. For the sake of her daughter, Joan sought help for her own drinking problem. "My daughter told me that I was a better mother when I was drunk. I guess I was nicer or something. But I think I was just so miserable when I was sober—drinking was sort of like escaping. When she said this, I knew I had a problem." After Joan started treatment for her alcohol problem, the assaults by her partner seemed to intensify. His jealous rages increased, as did his lack of control in general. "It's like he didn't want me to get sober or something."

One summer night, Joan went to see a movie with her friends. When they came out of the theater, her boyfriend was standing outside of a bar across the street. He came over and told her he wanted to talk to her. She went with him. They drove to a local park where he threw her out of the truck and began kicking and beating her. Her friends had followed them to the park, but did not get there in time to save Joan from sustaining three fractured ribs, a black eye, and several severe gashes and bruises on her body.

Joan sought refuge at the shelter, where she continued in treatment and counseling. She is not bitter and is remarkably confident. She plans to relocate to a nearby city to find employment to make a better life for herself and her daughter. "In my drinking days, I didn't know what I really wanted or who I really was. I could never identify my feelings. Maybe it was better that way then. But now I feel a lot better about myself, and I know that the violence wasn't my fault."

ALCOHOL USE AND FAMILY VIOLENCE

Similar to the association of alcohol use and homicide that we have observed in previous chapters, it is apparent that alcohol use was often a precursor to the partner violence experienced by the women I interviewed. Reiterating from Table 6.1, three-quarters of the women sampled from these battered women's shelters were admitted following an assault that occurred after the offender had been drinking. This is drastically higher than percentages found in the general population. For example, Kaufman and Straus (1990) report that only 24 percent of their nationally representative sample were under the influence of alcohol immediately prior to the act of spousal violence.

Even though these percentages are generally much lower in the general population, a number of investigators *have* found an association between alcohol and family violence for the population in general.[1]

Perhaps the most sophisticated study to date has been done by Kaufman and Straus (1987). Their findings reveal a strong link between alcohol use and physical abuse of wives, with the strongest relationship found to involve binge-drinking, blue-collar husbands who approve of violence.

Virtually all of the women I interviewed believed that alcohol was a precipitating factor in the assaults made on them. When I asked one woman what she would do to help combat spousal abuse in her community, she said, "The first thing I would do would be to start programs to treat alcoholism. That would be my main target. I don't think you can fix anything until you get that under control." This sentiment was confirmed by everyone whom I talked with, including social workers and counselors.

It is important to reiterate, however, that problems of alcohol abuse do not exist in a vacuum. Alcoholism among American Indians has been found to be associated with and intensified by an array of phenomena, including social disorganization, anomie, and alienation (Kraus & Buffler, 1979; Kahn, 1982). Others have cited a lack of social acceptance, unemployment, and underemployment (Frederick, 1973; Levy & Kunitz, 1974; Jarvis & Boldt, 1982). The director of one battered women's shelter states, "The alcohol is, of course, everpresent, and you wonder, Is alcohol the cause of the problems, or is it the result of everything that these people must live with like the unemployment? But this is not for us here to answer. We must deal with the violence, but we do know that alcohol certainly seems to enhance the violence."

Because alcohol use is a seemingly major problem in the American Indian population, and because preliminary investigations have found a strong link between alcohol use and domestic violence in this population, the primary research question that the last section of this chapter will address is this: To what extent does heavy drinking increase the probability of wife abuse among American Indian men?

Stress and Family Violence

Even though the family is often seen as a place where one can find respite from the tensions of the world, in reality it is a group with an inherently high level of conflict and stress.[2] Family members are often the scapegoats of the aggression that results from everyday stressors. This is especially the case with regard to American Indian families because of the many stressful events to which American Indians are subjected. While every family in this country is susceptible to stressful life events, American Indian families are particularly susceptible to those stressors involving support. For example, the family is expected to provide food and shelter. However, the reality for many American Indian families is that unemployment is everpresent and home may be simply "shelter" and nothing more. These conditions place tremendous stress on some American Indian families.

Most of the women I interviewed were unemployed at the time of the abuse, as were their partners. This condition alone brought undue amounts of stress into the relationship, particularly when there were children to care for.

One woman said, "He would be O.K. if he was working, but work was not always around. Then he would sit around the house and soon start drinking. I knew I was in for some trouble." Previous chapters, particularly Chapter 3, have already documented the hopelessness and hostility that unemployment and poverty can engender in individuals. While it is not clear to what extent this economic deprivation may have contributed to the violence these women experienced, it is not illogical to conjecture that its role was significant.

Research on the relationship of stress to family violence in the general population has found stress to be a significant predictor of violence between partners (Gabarino & Ebata, 1983; Straus, 1990). The last section of this chapter will also explore the degree to which stress has contributed to violence in American Indian families, net of other important factors such as alcohol use. Its focus will be the incidence and etiology of American Indian family violence, using the 1985 National Family Resurvey. We will begin with a brief description of this survey.

NATIONAL FAMILY VIOLENCE RESURVEY

Sample

The sample used for this portion of the chapter was based on the 1985 National Family Violence Resurvey (Straus and Gelles, 1990). Cases involving American Indians and non–American Indian Whites were drawn from this national probability sample. A total of 204 American Indian families was available in the Resurvey. In addition, a random sample of 2,007 non–American Indian Whites was selected here for purposes of comparison.

There are limitations, however, in using these data to study American Indian families. The first has to do with the question, Who is an American Indian? As discussed in Chapter 1, there are differing definitions of an American Indian. Respondents who self-classified themselves as American Indian represent the sample for this study. Therefore, it is important to reiterate that there are limitations to a study that globally refers to American Indians, just as there exists considerable diversity in homicide rates within this population. The findings of this chapter will undoubtedly exhibit unique variations at local tribal levels as well.

Violence Measures

Family violence was operationally defined using the Conflict Tactics Scales (CTS).[3] The CTS is designed to measure a variety of behaviors used in conflicts between family members during a reference period of twelve months. It asks respondents to recall the times "in the past year" when they and their partner "disagree on major decisions, get annoyed about something the other person does, or just have spats or fights because they're in a bad mood or tired or for some other reason." The instructions go on to say: "I'm going to read a list of some things that you and your partner might have done when you had a dispute and would like you to tell me for each one how often you did it in the past year." The list spans many techniques, including reasoning, verbal aggression, and finally physical aggression or "violence."

The CTS items are often subdivided into "minor" and "severe" violence. The minor violence items are as follows: threw something at the other family member; pushed, grabbed, or shoved; and slapped. The severe violence index measures assaults that have a relatively high probability of causing injury. The items are as follows: kicked, bit, or punched; hit or tried to hit with an object; beat up; choked; threatened with a knife or gun; and used a knife or gun.

Measure of Alcohol Consumption

The Drinking Index used in this chapter was developed by Kaufman and Straus (1987). Its purpose is to differentiate patterns *and* levels of drinking, and it was designed to identify binge patterns of drinking, which have been shown to be strongly related to domestic violence (Kaufman and Straus, 1987). The Drinking Index combines data from two survey questions:

(1) In general, how often do you consume alcoholic beverages—that is, beer, wine or liquor? never, less than 1 day a month, 1-3 days a month, 1-2 days a week, 3-4 days a week, 5-6 days a week, daily.

(2) On a day when you do drink alcoholic beverages, on the average, how many drinks do you have? By a "drink" we mean a drink with a shot of 1½ ounces of hard liquor, 12 ounces of beer, or 5 ounces of wine.

The frequency and amount data from these questions were used to develop six categories of drinking:

0 = *Abstinent:* Never drinks.

1 = *Low:* Drinks on infrequent occasions, ranging from less than once a month up to 1-2 times a week; never more than 1 drink at a time. Drinks less than once a month and no more than 2 drinks at a time.

2 = *Low Moderate:* Drinks from 1 to 3 times a month up to daily; never more than 2 drinks.

3 = *Low Binge:* Drinks less than once a month up to 1 to 2 times a week: 3-4 drinks a day.

4 = *High:* Drinks 3-4 times a week up to daily; 3 or more drinks a day.

5 = *Binge:* Drinks on infrequent occasions—once a month up to 1 to 2 times a week; 5 or more drinks a day.

Measure of Stress

The operationalization of stress used in this research focuses on the subjective experience of feeling stressed. The measure used as an indicator of stress is an additive index consisting of the responses to three items based on a five-point Likert Scale: (1) felt nervous or stressed, (2) felt difficulties were too great, and (3) could not cope.

Demographic Controls

In addition to the measures of drinking and stress, certain demographic control measures were included in the analysis because of their association with both ethnicity and family violence. Family income was used as an indicator of economic status. This variable was measured in four intervals ranging from the lowest category of zero to ten thousand dollars to the highest category of forty thousand dollars and over. The age of the respondent was also included as a control because the literature has documented its inverse relationshp with family violence (Stets and Straus, 1990; Suitor, Pillemer, and Straus, 1990).

Data Analyses

At the beginning of the next section, rates of family violence calculated by ethnicity provide an estimate of the incidence of spousal violence among American Indian families. For each measure of violence presented in this section (overall couple violence and husband-to-wife violence), respondents who had committed at least one act of violence were assigned a value of 1, and those who had committed no acts were coded as 0. These rates were then compared to a sample of non–American Indian White families.

The next part of the analysis will take a closer look at spousal violence in American Indian families. A multivariate analysis of the structural determinants of violence among American Indian couples is presented. Because the measures of violence are dichotomies, logistic regression rather than OLS regression was performed.[4]

INCIDENCE AND PREVALENCE RATES

The purposes of this section are to examine the magnitude of family violence in the American Indian population and to compare this to the rates of the non–American Indian White population. The demographic characteristics of the samples used are displayed in Table 6.2. From this, it can be seen that a larger percentage of American Indians reside in rural settings (41 percent) compared to Whites (29 percent). A greater percentage of American Indians is also represented in the lower income levels, with 15 percent of American Indian families earning $10,000 or less compared to only 9 percent of White families. Also, both American Indian husbands and wives are more often employed in blue-collar occupations compared to the White sample.

Couple Violence

The rates of spousal assault for American Indians and Whites are presented in Table 6.3. The first two rows in Table 6.3 give the rates of couple violence. The rate of 15.5 for any violence for the American Indian population indicates that over 15 percent of American Indian couples experienced an incident of physical violence during 1985. Applying this rate to the number of American Indian couples in the United States in 1985, we can estimate that approximately 37,000 couples experienced at least one act of violence during that year. This rate is somewhat higher than that found for the White population (14.8).

A substantial number of these assaults were severe, as indicated in the second row. Over 7 percent of these couples engaged in acts of violence that could have been potentially injurious, such as kicking, punching, and stabbing. Specifically, out of 36,940 couple assaults, approximately 18,000 could be considered severe assaults.

Husband-to-Wife Violence

The third and fourth rows in Table 6.3 present the rate and estimated number of assaults for acts of violence that were perpetrated by the husband. It can be seen that the rates for both any violence and severe violence are higher for American Indian populations than for White populations.

The rate of 12.2 per 100 couples for any act of violence indicates that just over 12 percent of American Indian husbands carried out one or more violent acts during 1985. What is even more troubling is the rate of severe violence. This indicates that more than 3 out of every 100 women were severely assaulted by their partner during the year of this study.

Table 6.2
Demographic Differences Between American Indians and Whites

Demographics	Percentage of:	
	Amer.Ind.	Whites
Region		
Northeast	13.2%	19.4%
North Central	27.5	26.8
South	45.6	34.6
West	13.7	19.2
Urban or Rural		
City	20.6	23.3
Suburb	38.7	47.6
Rural	40.7	29.0
Family Annual Income		
None – $10,000	15.3	8.6
$10,000 – $20,000	24.3	20.9
$20,000 – $40,000	44.0	43.4
$40,000 and over	16.4	27.0
Husband's Occup. Status		
Blue Collar	74.0	49.0
White Collar	26.0	51.0
Wife's Occup. Status		
Blue Collar	50.0	33.0
White Collar	50.0	67.0
Husband's Employment		
Full Time	71.2	77.4
Part Time	6.5	3.2
Unemployed, other	10.9	5.7
Retired	11.4	13.7
Wife's Employment		
Full Time	39.1	41.0
Part Time	9.6	13.4
Unemployed, other	46.2	37.4
Retired	5.1	8.3

Table 6.3
Annual Incidence Rates of Violence in American Indian and Non–American Indian White Families and Estimated Number of American Indian Cases Based on These Rates, 1985

Type of Intra-Family Violence	Rate per 100 Couples White	American Indian	Estimated Number of American Indians Assaulted Per Year*
VIOLENCE BETWEEN HUSBAND AND WIFE			
ANY violence during the yr (slap, push, etc.)	14.8	15.5	37,000
SEVERE violence (kick, punch, stab, etc.)	5.3	7.2	18,000
ANY violence by the HUSBAND	11.0	12.2	29,000
SEVERE violence by the HUSBAND ("wife beating")**	3.0	3.2	6,000

*The column giving the "Number Assaulted" was computed by multiplying the rates in this table by the 1980 Census Bureau estimate of the American Indian population.

**Because of the greater average size and strength of men, the acts in the severe violence list are likely to be more damaging when the assailant is the husband. To facilitate focusing on the rate of severe violence by husbands, the term "wife beating" has often been used to refer to this rate (Straus and Gelles, 1990).

Applying this percentage to the population at risk, an estimated 6,000 American Indian women were beaten by their partner in 1985.

These rates are presented graphically in Figure 6.1. This figure better illustrates the magnitude of differences found between American Indian and White rates of domestic violence. It can be seen that the American Indian rate of couple violence is 5 percent higher than the White rate. When this is limited to severe violence, American Indian families experience nearly 36 percent more assaultive behaviors than do White families. Similarly, when husband-to-wife violence is compared, any violence perpetrated by husbands is about 10 percent higher in American Indian families, and severe violence by American Indian husbands is 6 percent higher.

Problems of Underestimation

All of the rates in Table 6.3 should be regarded as "lower bound" estimates for several reasons. The first reason has to do with our sample of American Indians. Approximately half of American Indians live on reser-

Figure 6.1
Violence in American Indian and White Couples, 1985

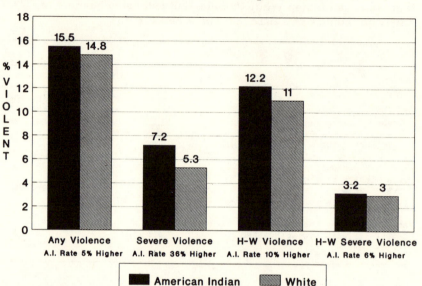

vations, while the other half reside in urban areas. This poses several problems with generalizing this sample to the entire population of American Indians. First, Census estimates indicate that, on many reservations, as many as 60 percent of the households do not have telephones. The sample for this study was obtained by using a random telephone survey. Consequently, the sample probably represents American Indians who reside in urban areas more than it does those who reside on reservations.

Reservation Indians have been found to be less fortunate than urban Indians in many respects. They suffer greater degrees of economic deprivation (Sorkin, 1976), more deaths resulting from alcoholism, and higher homicide and suicide rates (Kenen and Hammerslough, 1987). It is therefore possible that the estimates presented in this report are drastically lower than those that would be obtained if a representative sample of both reservation and urban American Indians were obtained.

Other reasons why these rates should be regarded as "lower bound" estimates are outlined by Straus, Gelles, and Steinmetz (1980, p. 35). Some family members may fail to report acts like slapping and pushing simply because it is a normal part of family life and is not noteworthy or dramatic enough to be remembered. On the other hand, some may not report an incident because of the shame involved, if one is the victim, or because of the guilt, if one is the offender. And, finally, because the sample consists exclusively of couples currently living together, previous marriages that may have included excessive violence (and therefore resulted in divorce) may have been missed.

DRINKING AND STRESS

This section will identify factors that are important in predicting spousal violence in the American Indian population. Using a sample of 204 American Indian families from the National Family Violence Resurvey, a statistical analysis is presented.

The first step in examining the drinking and violence connection was to compute wife abuse rates for each of the six types of drinkers identified by the Drinking Index. These rates are presented in Figure 6.2 and

Figure 6.2
Husband-to-Wife Violence as a Function of Drinking Type, 1985

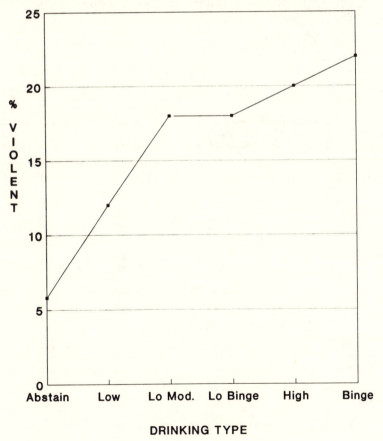

DRINKING TYPE

provide strong evidence of a linear association between drinking and wife abuse. The percentage of violent husbands rises dramatically from 5.8 percent for abstainers to a high of 22 percent for binge drinkers. From this, it appears that the higher and potentially more problematic the drinking level, the higher the rate of spousal violence perpetrated by the husband. It is important to note, however, that those who report abstaining from alcohol consumption do not have rates of violence equal to zero. The next step in exploring the relationship between drinking and spousal assault was to control for other important explanatory factors that might also contribute to levels of wife abuse.

Table 6.4 presents the results of logistic regression analyses for two models that predict levels of couple violence in general and also husband-to-wife violence for American Indians.

Part A of this table presents the results when estimating the probability of couple violence from all exogenous variables. It can be seen that the Drink Index was found to be a significant predictor of couple violence $(p = .005)$. As the frequency and intensity of drinking increased, so did

Table 6.4
Logistic Regression Results of Family Violence by Demographic Measures

Demographic Variable	Regression Coefficient	Standard Error	t	Level of Sig.
A. Couple Violence				
Age of respondent	-.079	.030	-2.582	.011
Urbanicity	.165	.348	.474	.635
Family annual income	.173	.097	1.773	.078
Drink Index	.547	.192	2.846	.005
Stress	.266	.192	3.288	.001
Constant	-4.01	1.905	-2.104	.036

N of Cases = 167, chi-square = 37.89, p < .0001

Demographic Variable	Regression Coefficient	Standard Error	t	Level of Sig.
B. Husband-to-Wife Violence				
Age of respondent	-.064	.030	-2.109	.037
Urbanicity	.006	.363	.018	.986
Family annual income	.054	.102	.528	.598
Drink Index	.352	.195	1.995	.051
Stress	.303	.083	3.643	.001
Constant	-1.866	1.503	-1.241	.216

N of Cases = 167, chi-square = 10.41, p < .034

incidents of violence within this sample of American Indians. Stress also had a significant relationship with couple violence (p = .001). As perceived levels of stress went up, so did the probability of violence between partners. The only other significant predictor in this model was age (p = .011). As age increased, the probability of couple violence decreased. This inverse relationship between age and violence has been extensively documented in the literature (Suitor, Pillemer, and Straus, 1990).

Part B of Table 6.4 presents results of the husband-to-wife violence analysis. Again, stress is a significant predictor of acts of violence perpetrated by the husband (p = .001), as is the Drink Index (p = .051). The demographic control of age is also significant (p = .037). So, similar to couple violence in general, as levels of both stress and drinking increase, so does the probability of husband-to-wife violence.

The results found here for American Indians are consistent with other studies that have examined the relationships among stress, alcohol, and family violence (Kaufman and Straus, 1987). Assaults between partners are more likely to occur when there is a tendency to consume large quantities of alcohol. This relationship is true of stress as well. As levels of perceived stress increase, so does the probability of family violence.

A different way to illustrate the fact that acts of violence increase at a greater rate when a husband engages in binge drinking is through the use of a conditional effect plot. Figure 6.3 presents the effects of stress on acts of husband-to-wife violence at three levels of drinking behavior: abstinent, low moderate drinking, and binge drinking. From the graph, one can easily ascertain that as levels of perceived stress increase, levels of assaultive behavior increase as well. However, the steeper slope for binge drinking indicates that this relationship is intensified when the husband is a binge drinker. That is, those who have many drinks when they do drink, but who tend to drink infrequently (once a month up to one to two times a week) have a greater probability of assaulting their wives when under stress than do those who abstain from drinking alcohol.

What is perplexing about the results, however, is that no significant relationship was found between income level and American Indian spousal violence. It should be noted that a preliminary bivariate analysis (not reported here) of this same data with chi-square revealed a significant relationship between poverty and domestic violence, using the income measure included in the models and including a dichotomous variable of blue-collar and white-collar status. That is, as income level increased, the probability of spousal violence decreased. The spousal violence rates were also significantly higher for blue-collar workers than for white-collar workers. When simultaneously controlling for other variables, such as alcohol use, stress, and age, however, measures of economic standing appear to drop out.

Figure 6.3
Probability of Husband-to-Wife Violence as a Logit Function of
Perceived Stress at Three Levels of Drinking

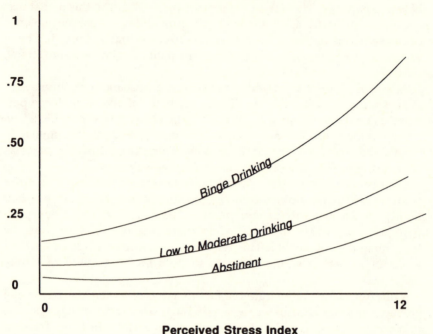

Perceived Stress Index

SUMMARY

This chapter has examined violence in American Indian families. Fieldwork at three battered women's shelters located on reservations revealed that, in the typical scenario of wife beating, the husband or boyfriend goes out with his friends and drinks too much. Then he makes faulty assumptions and goes into a jealous rage, which usually culminates in an assault on his partner.

The second section of the chapter examined the incidence and etiology of violence in American Indian families, using a nationally representative sample of American Indians (204) and a comparison sample of non–American Indian Whites (2,007). The incidence rates of American Indian couple violence were estimated to be 15.5 per 100 American Indian couples. These acts of spousal assault were found to be higher in the American Indian sample than in the White comparison group. This suggests that over 37,000 American Indian couples experience violence every year. Further, 18,000 of the assaults are severe enough to be potentially injurious. Assaults perpetrated by the husband were estimated to affect approximately 29,000 American Indian women, with 6,000 of these categorized as "wife beating." Because of sample limitations and because of the virtual certainty that not every respondent was completely frank in describing violent incidents, these numbers should be regarded as minimum estimates. These are alarming numbers, considering that they are estimated for a population of only about 1.4 million people.

After controlling for economic deprivation, age, and urbanicity, it was found that higher rates of both alcohol consumption and perceived stress significantly increase the probability of couple violence in general and of husband-to-wife assaults.

While the evidence just presented indicates that there is a strong linkage among alcohol consumption, stress, and violence in American Indian families, the number of cases for analysis is important to consider. This analysis is based on a relatively small number of American Indian families (N = 204) and an even smaller number of these families exhibiting spousal violence. This fact, in addition to the sample problems outlined earlier, should compel the reader to be cautious when generalizing these results to the population of American Indian families in general.

It is clear that violence is a problem that is eminently important in American Indian families, just as it is in all families. Spousal assault in American Indian populations must be recognized as a serious problem. Communities need to implement educational programs that focus attention on the issue. The immediate need is for more funding to assist abused American Indian women and their children because their safety is undoubtedly at stake.

To reiterate, results from this analysis should be regarded as tentative. Future research should focus not only on domestic violence in American Indian families, but also on understanding American Indian families in general. Straus (1986) explains: "What we know about Indian families is fragmented, anecdotal, descriptive, and often overpowered by poor understanding of the particular cultures being studied" (p. 345). With regard to domestic violence, future research should focus on exploring such violence within more homogeneous units, such as specific tribal and reservation communities. Urban and rural differences also need to be considered. American Indian intrafamily violence is a complex and multifaceted issue. There are so many gaps in our understanding of how contemporary American Indian family formations actually function that this chapter raises more questions than it actually answers. It is hoped that it will be a catalyst for future work in this area.

NOTES

1. Gelles, 1974; Rosenbaum & O'Leary, 1981; Coleman & Straus, 1983; Kaufman & Straus, 1987.

2. For a detailed theoretical case for this view, see Farrington, 1980; Straus, 1990.

3. For a detailed description of the CTS, see Straus, 1979, 1990.

4. The logistic regression method applies a nonlinear transformation so that the dependent variable is no longer the dichotomous occurrence of Y. The equation estimates are based on the logarithm of the ratio between the probability $Y = 1$ and the probability $Y \neq 1$ (Aldrich & Nelson, 1984, pp. 31-33).

Chapter 7

When Aggression Is Turned Inward

Durkheim was one of the first social scientists to study rates of suicide. He clearly defined suicide as "all causes of death resulting directly or indirectly from a positive or negative act of the victim himself which he knows will produce this result" ([1897] 1951, p. 44). According to Durkheim, suicide is the ultimate act of defiance. With regard to the American Indian population, LaFromboise and Bigfoot (1988) give a more graphic description:

It reflects the hopelessness of trapped and imprisoned souls. It is an unwillingness to continue suffering. . . . According to many American Indians, whose lives have been affected by the governmental goal of assimilating them into the general ethos of American life, suicide could be construed as the ultimate act of freedom. It is an act that defies governmental control and challenges the dominant society to face up to its irresponsibility in meeting treaty agreements for health, education and welfare.

Chapter 2 presented the national suicide rates for American Indians, Whites, and Blacks for the years 1965-1983. From this analysis, as well as other data from the National Center for Health Statistics (1987), it appears that American Indians have, on average, maintained the highest rates of suicide for this time period. While it is the eighth leading cause of death for the general population it is one of the leading causes of death for American Indians, particularly young Indian males.

Interest in American Indian suicide did not burgeon until the middle of this century (Fenton, 1941; Devereaux, 1942). Much of this early work was conducted on a tribal-specific level and was primarily involved with issues of incidence. This literature produced alarming statistics, which seemed to indicate that suicide had reached epidemic proportions in most American Indian communities. Later, other research uncovered the nuances inherent in aggregate-level suicide statistics. It was found that most tribes had their own unique pattern of suicide. In fact, studies revealed that suicide rates varied between some tribal groups by as much as 150 per 100,000 population.[1]

Despite extreme differences in tribal suicide behavior and rates, it appears that American Indian suicide is primarily a phenomenon of the young. American Indian suicide rates peak in young adulthood and decrease with age. This is much different from suicide in the general population, where rates peak in both adolescence and old age. It has also been documented that the majority of American Indian suicides are committed by males through the use of a firearm or hanging. Suicides by American Indian females are more often made through drug overdoses and more often remain attempts rather than resulting in death (Berlin, 1986, 1987; McIntosh, 1984). And similar to the findings presented earlier in this book on contributors of homicide and family violence, a vast majority of American Indian suicides appear to be related to heavy alcohol use.

THE ETIOLOGY OF AMERICAN INDIAN SUICIDE

Many social factors have been found to be associated with high suicide rates in American Indian populations. We have seen in previous chapters that social disorganization and economic deprivation are important contributors to high levels of lethal violence directed toward others. The literature on the etiology of suicide seems to suggest that these social conditions also affect the propensity for American Indian populations to direct aggression inward in the form of suicide.

After conducting extensive postmortem interviews with the families and significant others of American Indian adolescent suicides in the Southwest, Dizmang and others (1974) found that a much higher percentage of suicide victims had indicators of social disorganization present in their lives than did a matched control group. For example, 70 percent of the suicides had more than one significant caretaker before the age of fifteen compared to only 15 percent of the controls. Fifty percent of the suicide group had experienced two or more losses by divorce or desertion compared to 10 percent of the control group. And 60 percent of the suicides had attended boarding school before the ninth grade compared to 27.5 percent of the controls.[2]

Other researchers have emphasized the cultural milieus that may contribute to high levels of suicide and suicide attempts. These studies have investigated the degree to which a tribal group's level of stability or integration is related to suicide. This research indicates, at least for southwestern tribes and pueblos, that by maintaining tribal tradition, a level of integration is achieved through stable religious traditions and extended families. This integration tends to decrease rates of suicide. Conversely, the more unstable or in transition (i.e., in a process of acculturation) a tribal community is, the greater its suicide rate tends to be.[3] Others have added that an environment in transition is also likely to increase culture conflict (see Chapter 3 for a discussion).

While many investigators have noted these causal factors, none has employed multivariate statistics to test the hypothesis that reservation-to-reservation differences in such factors as social disorganization and poverty affect the suicide differentials that exist among reservation communities. Of course, it would have been ideal to statistically control for alcohol consumption levels in reservation communities, but there was no suitable indicator for this. This chapter will formally test three hypotheses:

1. The higher the level of social disorganization within a reservation community, the higher the rate of suicide.
2. The higher the level of economic deprivation within a reservation community, the higher the rate of suicide.
3. The more traditional and integrated a reservation community, the lower the rate of suicide.

Unlike the chapters that preceded this, the analysis of suicide presented here relies primarily on quantitative methods. While I have encountered several cases of suicide in my field experience, the numbers are not sufficient for me to make any generalizations with regard to causality. But before moving on to the statistical analysis, I want to give the reader two case studies that will illustrate the devastating reality of suicide for many American Indians and the families who survive them. The first involves a suicide attempt by a young American Indian woman. To protect the anonymity of the individuals involved, I will use the pseudonym Alice when referring to her. The other case involves a completed suicide by a young American Indian male, whom I will call John.

Alice

Alice was born on a reservation in the early 1970s. Her childhood was characterized by relative stability compared to many on her reservation. Her parents were community business owners who provided Alice with essentially all the material things a child could want. Family photo albums are filled with pictures that depict a young Alice with a smile from ear to ear.

Junior high school was an extension of everything that characterized grade school—good grades, many extracurricular activities, and involvement with the church youth group. High school, however, was a different story. Shortly after beginning her freshman year, Alice acquired a somewhat different set of friends. She no longer had time to attend the activities of the church youth group, and her grades began to fall. By her sophomore year, Alice was spending little time on anything but partying with her friends. When not coming home at night began to be the rule, rather than the exception, her parents intervened by sending her to a parochial school. This, however, only led to runaway episodes, during which Alice would not return to the school until she was forced to.

By her junior year in high school, any resemblance that Alice had to her childhood past had disappeared. She was not only drinking, but also taking other drugs. Those around her soon realized that until her addiction problem was treated, her life would never return to normal. Because of truancy and other minor infractions, Alice was ordered by the court to attend a treatment program for alcoholic teenagers. This three-week program only seemed to infuriate Alice, and, upon release, she ran away for over two weeks.

After she returned, her parents remember an almost calm time. Alice had started going out with a man who was four years older than she was, and this appeared to have a stabilizing effect on her. Whether it was because he was older and somewhat more responsible or simply because he provided security for her did not matter. They did not question the origin, but were only thankful for the reappearance of a less angry and more loving daughter.

They had this peace for only six months until this, too, was shattered by a call from the hospital emergency room. Alice had taken an overdose of drugs and had been rushed to the hospital after being found by a friend. The overdose had apparently occurred after Alice and her boyfriend had a fight and ended their relationship.

Alice did not die. Today she exists in an almost vegetablelike state. Her parents are her primary caregivers. Reality for Alice is now staring off into space in a room that is filled with pictures from her past.

John

John's early life was characterized by instability. He lived primarily with his mother who moved back and forth between the reservation and a nearby urban area. At an early age, John's brother remembers John being involved in escapist behavior, such as sniffing glue and drinking when he could get alcohol.

When he had reached junior high school, his grandmother intervened and enrolled him in school on the reservation where he was to live with her. Because he had already established a peer network on the reservation, his life changed very little. He did attend school, but his grades were mediocre at best.

In high school, athletics soon replaced drugs as John's extracurricular activity. Although weekends were still characterized by drinking binges with his friends, basketball was his passion during the winter and was replaced by track and field in the spring. He excelled in sports, and during the school year he was popular both in the community and among his peers.

During the spring of his senior year, John began experiencing episodes of depression. He was going "steady" with a girl who was younger than he was, and he was often taking first place in cross-country track meets. But he was still "having problems" that no one seemed able to help him with. The spring of his senior year was characterized by extreme highs followed by extreme lows.

It was during one of the low valleys that he was found in his car with a bullet hole through his head and a shoulder gun beside him. Also on the floor of the car was an almost empty bottle of whiskey. No one has an explanation. He was experiencing trouble with his girlfriend, but most believe that he was simply having trouble dealing with the fact that his life in the limelight of high school would soon be over. And the reality that awaited him was most likely that of unemployment and poverty.

METHODS FOR QUANTITATIVE ANALYSIS

The analysis that follows was performed on 120 counties that are totally or partially located on reservation land. County-level independent variables were obtained from the Census Subject Reports of American Indians, Eskimos, and Aleuts on Identified Reservations and in the Historic Areas of Oklahoma (U.S. Bureau of the Census, 1980). While in Chapter 4 indexes designed to measure the degree of both social disorganization and poverty within reservation communities were constructed, preliminary analysis here found individual indicators to be better predictors of suicide.

The data obtained from the Census for independent variables were then matched to American Indian suicide rates, which were calculated from county-level data obtained from the Indian Health Service of the Department of Health and Human Services for the years 1980-1987.

Independent Variables

Social Disorganization. The indicator used to measure social disorganization is the percentage of American Indians who did not live on their current reservation in 1979 or 1980—the mobility rate. Reiterating from

Chapter 4, the mobility rate within a community has been documented by other research as contributing to the disorganization of a community. The change in the residential population diminishes the sense of attachment to community norms and, therefore, reduces the ability of established institutions to regulate social behavior.

Economic Deprivation. Three indicators were included in the analysis that are intended to measure the extent of economic deprivation within reservation communities: (1) the percentage of American Indian families below the Social Security Administration's defined poverty level, (2) the percentage of American Indians unemployed, and (3) the percentage of American Indians aged sixteen to nineteen who are not enrolled in school and who are not high school graduates (i.e., the dropout rate). Each of these indicators is believed to measure different spheres of economic deprivation.

Traditionalism/Acculturation. As noted earlier, communities that are in transition (i.e., in a process of acculturation) and that are less traditional appear to exhibit higher rates of suicide, while more traditional groups have lower rates of suicide. Westlake Van Winkle and May (1986) have postulated that the way to determine the level of acculturation of American Indian groups is to look at the factor of White contact. Advancing a notion from Linton (1972), these authors state that "the contact between Native Americans and Whites [is] an example of directed culture change because the Whites were the dominant group actively and intentionally interfering with the Indian culture. With culture change, some Native American groups experienced losses of cultural traits without replacement as well as the inhibition of preexisting culture patterns" (p. 307). Westlake Van Winkle and May found that the level of acculturation operationalized in this way increased the rates of suicide within tribes and pueblos in the Southwest. This research postulates the same. Acculturation will be operationalized as the intensity of White contact.

Specifically, the percentage of American Indians will be used to measure the degree of White contact. In this way, the higher the percentage of American Indians within a reservation community, the higher the level of traditionality. The lower the percentage of American Indians, the higher the degree of White contact and presumed acculturation. As measured here, the percentage of American Indians should have a negative relationship with the suicide rates. That is, as the level of traditionality increases, the level of suicide should decrease.

Controls. The percentage of the American Indian population that is aged eighteen to twenty-four is included in the analysis as a demographic control. This is an important statistical control in an analysis of suicide within this population because, as noted earlier, suicide rates tend to be highest for this age group.

Dependent Variable

Suicide Rate. The suicide rates used in this analysis are presented in Table 7.1. The incidents of suicide used in calculating these rates cover the entire 1980-1987 period, not individual years. This procedure was used to reduce the influence of random aberrations in year-to-year estimates, in addition to reducing the unreliability of rates based on low frequencies. The total American Indian suicide rate at the county level was calculated by employing both denominators and numerators obtained from the Indian Health Service. The formula for rate calculation was as follows:

$$[(I/P) \times 100,000]/8$$

where I = the total number of incidents of suicide in that county and P = the total American Indian population of that county. The division by eight indicates that the rates are calculated over the entire 1980-1987 period and then expressed on a per-year basis.

RESULTS

Bivariate Analysis

Table 7.2 presents the correlation matrix of all independent variables with each other and with the American Indian suicide rate. The variables that have the strongest correlation with suicide are the percentage of the population that is American Indian and the percentage of American Indians who are unemployed (both $r = .18$). The high school dropout rate is not much lower, with a coefficient of .17, followed by the percentage of the population aged eighteen to twenty-four (.15), the percentage of the population below the poverty level (.09), and the mobility rate in the community (.07).

All of these variables exhibit positive correlations with the suicide rate. This contradicts the third hypothesis, which stated that the more traditional a reservation community is (the higher the percentage of American Indians is), the lower the suicide rate would be. The correlation results indicate that the higher the percentage of American Indians within a reservation community is, the higher the suicide rate is. Because this was our indicator of acculturation, we can infer that as the degree of traditionality increases, so does the level of suicide within reservation communities. This is contrary to our original hypothesis.

How can we interpret this? Others have alluded to the fact that traditional communities may also have deleterious effects on suicide. For example, Berlin (1987) states:

Table 7.1

Reservation-County-Level Rank Order Listing of Suicide Rates, 1980-1987 (N = 100 Reservation Counties)

Rank	COUNTY	SUICIDE RATE	Rank	COUNTY	SUICIDE RATE
1	Snohomish	2.88	51	Gila	21.04
2	Tulare	4.78	52	Beltrami	21.07
3	Swain	4.79	53	Navajo	21.32
4	Corson	4.86	54	Maricopa	21.71
5	Thurston	4.94	55	Otero	22.05
6	Thurston	4.94	56	Lake	22.52
7	Blaine	5.35	57	Washington	23.00
8	Franklin	5.90	58	Mason	23.61
9	PrinceofWales	7.18	59	Brown	24.45
10	Osage	7.67	60	Mendocino	25.03
11	NezPerce	8.59	61	Sioux	25.38
12	Imperial	8.82	62	St.Louis	25.47
13	Fresno	8.98	63	Hill	25.63
14	DelNorte	9.12	64	Lyman	25.96
15	Jackson	10.03	65	Knox	26.37
16	Riverside	10.05	66	Sawyer	26.50
17	Yellowstone	10.45	67	RioAriba	28.13
18	MCKinley	10.48	68	Pinal	28.30
19	Coconino	10.68	69	Hendry	29.41
20	LaPlata	10.81	70	Inyo	29.98
21	Ashland	11.21	71	Skagit	32.08
22	Menominee	11.89	72	Umatilla	32.28
23	SanJuan	11.95	73	Rosebud	33.89
24	Clark	12.03	74	Glacier	35.15
25	Apache	12.42	75	Benson	35.41
26	Graham	13.27	76	Montezuma	36.38
27	Rolette	13.43	77	Pima	36.88
28	Sonoma	13.71	78	Ferry	36.98
29	Becker	13.76	79	Glades	37.31
30	CharlesMix	13.97	80	Buffalo	37.51
31	Whatcom	14.71	81	Washoe	37.94
32	Cattaraugus	14.75	82	Valencia	38.37
33	Bernalillo	14.77	83	Taos	38.94
34	Dewey	15.23	84	Wasco	39.12
35	Leake	15.55	85	Yuma	40.62
36	Stevens	16.09	86	Yakima	41.07
37	BigHorn	16.19	87	Elko	41.39
38	Jackson	16.32	88	Marshall	42.66
39	CarsonCity	16.38	89	Newton	48.08
40	Humboldt	17.00	90	Yavopai	49.29
41	SanJuan	17.01	91	Day	51.65
42	Missoula	17.42	92	Okanogan	55.69
43	Pierce	17.98	93	Lewis	56.82
44	Roosevelt	18.37	94	Burnett	59.67
45	King	18.49	95	Bingham	61.66
46	Pondera	18.55	96	Jefferson	65.26
47	Humboldt	18.66	97	Nye	67.93
48	Brown	19.11	98	Mohave	89.46
49	Bannock	19.58	99	Fremont	96.03
50	Neshoba	19.93	100	Douglas	120.77

Table 7.2
Correlation Matrix of the Total American Indian Suicide Rate
and American Indian–Specific Independent Variables, 1980-1987
(N = 100 Reservation Counties)

	1.	2.	3.	4.	5.	6.	7.
1. Suicide	1.0						
2. % 18-24	.15	1.0					
3. % Unemployed	.18	-.12	1.0				
4. % Dropouts	.17	.21	.13	1.0			
5. % Poor	.09	.09	.16	.33	1.0		
6. % Moved	.07	.02	.05	.02	-.23	1.0	
7. % Amer.Ind.	.18	.05	.04	.06	.36	-.40	1.0

Traditional communities, however, may impose old values on adolescents and young adults that may also lead to suicides or suicide attempts. For instance, an important American Indian value is that people should not strive to be better than others and thus cause others to lose face. In school and even in athletic events, being singled out as a superior student or athlete may bring ostracism or even physical chastisement from the peer group. Thus, at times, traditional tribes' values may be used to the detriment of their young people. (p. 226)

From this analysis, it appears that the traditionality of a reservation community does *not* ameliorate the effects of other conditions that may be present, such as unemployment and poverty; rather, it appears to exacerbate the problem. Of course, the percentage of the population that is American Indian is not a perfect indicator of the traditional status of a community. It might possibly be reflecting other structural or cultural circumstances that are not included in the model, such as culture conflict. For example, with a greater percentage of American Indians in a community, there is indeed a greater likelihood that those residents will develop a stronger Indian identity. But this cultural identity may, in turn, increase the perceived conflict that exists when one attempts to adopt the ways of the "dominant society," while still maintaining his or her cultural heritage. Thus, the higher the percentage of American Indians in the population, the greater the level of perceived culture conflict, and the greater the chance of suicide.

Before making a final judgment about this relationship, however, it is important to perform a multivariate regression analysis. In this way, we will be able to determine the extent to which each of these variables contributes to the suicide rates, net of each other.

Multivariate Analysis

The results of the ordinary least squares regression analysis are presented in Table 7.3. It appears that each of our measures of economic deprivation has a significant impact on the suicide rate within a reservation community. If we were to use a one-tailed t test with an alpha of .05, the unemployment rate, the high school dropout rate, and the percentage below the poverty level each contributes significantly to the suicide rate. As these indicators of economic deprivation increase within a reservation community, so does the suicide rate. Our measure of social disorganization, the mobility rate into a community, did not have a significant impact on the suicide rate while holding the other variables constant. The percentage of the population that is American Indian retained a positive, but insignificant relationship with suicide in this analysis as well.

It appears that environments riddled with poverty and deprivation also contribute to aggression, which is turned inward in the form of suicide. These impoverished environments thus appear conducive to both self- and other-directed forms of violence. There may be communities that are in such an extreme state of deprivation that there exists a propensity for individuals to act aggressively both toward others and toward themselves. This idea was alluded to in Chapter 2 as well. One way to empirically test this notion is to determine the relationship that

Table 7.3

Regression Analysis of All Independent Variables Predicting American Indian Suicide, 1980-1987 (N = 100 Reservation Counties)

	b	SE(b)	t	Significance
% 18-24	.389	.441	.882	.380
% Moved	.494	.406	1.21	.226
% Unemployed	.251	.145	2.08	.043
% Dropouts	.285	.206	1.72	.087
% Amer. Ind.	.849	.420	2.02	.046
% Poor	.399	.196	2.00	.047

exists between homicide rates and suicide rates within reservation communities. The correlation between these two rates is .34. This indicates a relatively strong relationship. In fact, this bivariate relationship is stronger than any relationship found between suicide and each of our other independent variables. To determine the effects of homicide, however, net of our other indicators, we must incorporate the homicide rate into our regression model predicting suicide rates.

The results of the regression analysis that includes the homicide rate are presented in Table 7.4. Here we see that two of our indicators of poverty are still significant predictors of suicide, net of the homicide rate. As the levels of unemployment and absolute poverty increase within a community, the suicide rate also increases. The high school dropout rate, as well as the mobility rate, fails to reach significance when we control for the homicide rate.

Because the homicide rate is significant, net of these variables, this validates our contention. Indeed, it appears that some reservation communities are in such a state of deprivation that the frustration experienced by its residents is manifested in acts of both internal and external aggression. In fact, when we list the reservation counties with the highest suicide rates and those with the highest homicide rates, we see that many counties appear on both lists. For example, the fifteen reservation counties with the highest rates of homicide and suicide are presented in Table 7.5. Here we see that several of the counties—Douglas, Marshall, Newton, and Lewis—appear on the lists for both suicide and homicide. It is beyond the scope of this chapter to perform the kind of in-depth his-

Table 7.4
Regression Analysis of All Independent Variables Predicting American Indian Suicide, Including the Homicide Rate, 1980-1987 (N = 100 Reservation Counties)

	b	SE(b)	t	Significance
% 18-24	.289	.451	.703	.410
% Moved	.394	.416	1.23	.227
% Unemployed	.302	.134	2.24	.027
% Dropouts	.161	.192	.837	.405
% Amer. Ind.	.598	.363	1.64	.103
% Poor	.448	.182	2.46	.015
Homicide Rate	.414	.107	3.87	.001

Table 7.5
**Rank Order Listing of the Fifteen Reservation Counties
with the Highest Rates of Suicide and Homicide**

Rank	County	Suicide Rate	County	Homicide Rate
1	Yakima	41.07	Imperial	50.41
2.	Elko	41.39	Swain	54.80
3.	Marshall	42.66	Newton	54.95
4.	Newton	48.08	Kootnai	59.15
5.	Yavopai	49.29	Knox	60.28
6.	Day	51.65	Todd	61.98
7.	Okanogan	55.69	Polk	63.21
8.	Lewis	56.82	Lewis	64.94
9.	Burnett	59.67	Rosebud	71.93
10.	Bingham	61.66	Corson	72.18
11.	Jefferson	65.26	Sauk	73.26
12.	Nye	67.93	Marshall	97.51
13.	Mohave	89.46	Douglas	103.52
14.	Fremont	96.03	Harney	127.55
15.	Douglas	120.77	Idaho	140.06

torical analysis that would be necessary to describe these reservation communities in detail. From the analysis here, however, it seems reasonable to conclude that our earlier contention is plausible. Because economic deprivation significantly predicts levels of both suicide and homicide, and because suicide and homicide rates are also significantly related to each other within communities, this indicates that some communities exist in such a state of despair and deprivation that destructive acts directed both toward others and toward the self appear to flourish.

SUMMARY

This chapter has examined the etiology of American Indian suicide through a reservation-county-level analysis. It was found that economic deprivation has a significant and positive impact on suicide within reservation communities. As the unemployment, dropout, and poverty rates increased within a reservation community, so did the suicide rate. When the homicide rate was also included in the predictive model, the rates of unemployment and income below the poverty level remained significant, but the high school dropout rate did not. The homicide rate had the strongest relationship to the suicide rate within a reservation community.

Reservation communities that are characterized by a high rate of economic deprivation also appear to be environments conducive to violence that is directed both toward others and toward the self. But generalizations should be drawn cautiously from these analyses. Research that investigates American Indian suicide with multivariate statistics is virtually nonexistent. The analysis here should be viewed as exploratory until more refined measures and models are developed through future research. Future research should investigate the cultural and structural milieus that exist in reservation communities where high rates of homicide and suicide coexist. What are the histories of these communities? Is extreme economic deprivation a sufficient, but not necessary element in creating these brutal environments? Do the residents of some communities have a higher probability of directing their aggressions outward toward others, while the residents of other communities inhibit these aggressions? Each of these questions suggests important areas of inquiry for future research.

It is apparent that suicide is related to structural circumstances within communities, such as unemployment and poverty. When communities provide little opportunity for economic self-sufficiency, frustrations appear to be manifested in acts of violence. These acts appear to be non-discriminatory and are directed both toward the self in acts of suicide and toward others in acts of assault that are often lethal.

NOTES

1. May & Dizmang, 1974; Berlin, 1987; McIntosh, 1980-1981; Westlake Van Winkle, & May, 1986. For a review of the literature see Willard, 1979 and Peters, 1981.

2. For others who note this see Johnson & Johnson, 1965; Townsley & Goldstein, 1977; Carlson & Cantwell, 1982.

3. Levy & Kunitz, 1971; May & Dizmang, 1974; Web & Willard, 1975; Shore & Manson, 1981; Westlake Van Winkle & May, 1986. For discussion of this see Berlin, 1986.

Chapter 8

Policy Implications

Abstract theories create abstract action. Lumping together the variety of tribal problems and seeking the demonic principle at work which is destroying Indian people may be intellectually satisfying. But it does not change the real situation. By concentrating on great abstractions, [social scientists] have unintentionally removed many young Indians from the world in which problems are solved to lands of make believe.

Vine Deloria, Jr. (1988)

The first step in developing theory is understanding a social phenomenon—documenting its existence and determining the factors that are related to this existence. We have seen that many social and personal conditions are related to the violence present in American Indian communities. It is hoped that what has been learned in the preceding pages of this book will be used to inform policy aimed at the prevention of this violence. As Deloria so eloquently expressed it in the passage quoted above, the development and testing of theory should not be divorced from the workings of the real world. The last thing that I want to produce from this research is an abstract theory that could go on to create abstract action. To prevent the implications of this research from getting lost, the purpose of this chapter is to provide a clear and unambiguous agenda for action.

This book has examined both the incidence and the etiology of three forms of violence within the American Indian population: homicide, domestic violence, and suicide. It was found that some reservation communities have staggering suicide and homicide rates. Consequently, it is clear that the lives of many American Indian youth may too often be cut short by violent death. While the results from comparable analyses of different samples will undoubtedly vary among more homogeneous tribal units, I believe the findings are generalizable to the entire Indian population. When a people is given little economic or political power, the frustration that this powerlessness engenders has similar effects, *regardless* of tribal affiliation. When a young Indian male or female perceives little opportunity for the future and no hope of escaping a cycle of poverty, the deleterious consequences of this are the same whether he or she is a registered member of the Navajo nation or of the Sioux. What we have is a generation of American Indians at risk.

It should be apparent that just as the causes of violence we have examined within this book are numerous, so, too, will it take an integrated and varied response in the form of policy prevention strategies to effectively deal with these problems. In addition, it should be understood that these problems cannot be solved by directing our efforts only at their surface manifestations. The problem of alcoholism does not persist apart from its more fundamental economic and political origins. For example, alcoholism prevention programs will not help a community unless we also provide economic opportunity and instill hope for the future. I want to begin my discussion with general recommendations and then move on to more specific policy implications.

SOVEREIGNTY AND SELF-DETERMINATION

One of the primary factors related to each of the three forms of violence analyzed in this book is economic deprivation. Creating policies that permit all American Indian communities to have the opportunity to become economically viable seems to be an urgent priority. But before we talk about these policies, what is the larger picture? What are the real conditions behind this deprivation and poverty? In 1989, the National Congress of American Indians concluded that tribal sovereignty must be retained if American Indians are going to lift themselves out of the economic depression in which they find themselves. F. Browning Pipestem, who was a Congress participant, stated, "The process of tribal sovereignty is what's going to carry us into the future. Tribal sovereignty is the last plane out of Casablanca for tribes. It is the last plane out of poverty and unemployment" (*Rapid City Journal*, Oct. 4, 1989). By its very nature, the concept of sovereignty connotes self-determination for American Indian people. Simply stated, it is the freedom to control their own lives—to manage their own affairs. But it is a freedom barely noticed because it is taken for granted in the White world.

Although the American Indian Self-Determination and Education Assistance Act, passed in 1975, has given tribal governments increased responsibility and administrative power, the problem of sovereignty still persists. This demand for self-determination is played out in many ways today. For example, many tribes are demanding that violated treaties be upheld. In constitutional terms, treaties are supposedly synonymous with the law of the land. But in practical terms, the vast majority of treaties entered into with our government by Indian nations are increasingly a matter of hostile contention between American Indians and their opposition (local and state authorities, business interests, White neighbors, and so forth). Some tribes are fighting for such things as fishing rights, while others are fighting to reclaim land bases that were taken from them.

An illustration of the lack of real sovereignty in the lives of American Indians is the case of the Lake Superior Chippewa. The Chippewa ceded land to the United States under treaties signed in 1836, 1837, 1842, and 1854, but retained the right to harvest resources on that land (to hunt, fish, and gather on that land). Even though the legal validity of these rights has recently been affirmed by federal court decisions, there is often a large gap between this and the personal validity of these rights for the Chippewa. For example, when they attempt to exercise their rights by spearfishing on northern Wisconsin lakes, they are often met by sometimes violent antitreaty protesters. When they attempted to fish in the spring of 1989, they were met with protesters screaming "Save a Walleye. Spear a pregnant squaw," and many protesters carried spears topped with fake Indian heads to illustrate their animosity.[1] This pointed display of racial animus is, unfortunately, not an isolated case. Almost everywhere that tribes are trying to claim treaty rights or land, displays such as this are more often the rule on the part of Whites, rather than the exception.

RACISM

Racism, prejudice, and discrimination are other evils that impede the advancement of American Indians. Beyond the possible discriminatory imposition of the law that was discussed in Chapter 5, many Indians must exist in an environment in which they are negatively stereotyped and devalued as individuals. This racism spans the spectrum from racism that has become institutionalized to acts on the individual level that are just as devastating in their effects. Let me illustrate incidents of both.

In writing about internal colonialism, Thomas (1975) emphasizes that while many of the intentions behind federal programs are benevolent, their effects are more often negative and result in such things as institutional racism. For example, the Bureau of Indian Affairs (BIA) was established in 1824 by the federal government to manage most tribal affairs. Today, one of the principal programs of the BIA administers and manages millions of acres of land held in trust for Indians by the United States. It also works with tribal governments to help provide a variety of local services, including social services, police protection, and road maintenance. Under the governance of the BIA then, the leadership in tribal groups still comes from *outside* of the group. However benevolent the BIA was intended to be, the structure has often plagued Indian advancement and self-determination. For example, on the Pine Ridge Reservation in South Dakota, the few small industries that exist are accountable to the BIA—*not* to the tribe. Indian businesses cannot get loans from private banks because the land is held in trust. Further, most of the land is leased to White ranchers. Consequently, the majority of the Sioux end up as migrant workers, unskilled workers in low-paying government jobs, or social welfare recipients. This structure helps keep the Sioux people out of the mainstream economy and, in a larger sense, has forced this tribe to become dependent on a primarily White bureaucracy.

Racism exists on a more micro level as well. As anyone who has lived on or near a reservation as I have can attest, there are countless examples of everyday acts of racism and discrimination. These acts include verbal taunts, jeers, jokes, and racial slurs, which usually stem from prejudice. Parrillo (1985) has defined prejudice as an attitudinal "system of negative beliefs, feelings, and action-orientations regarding a certain group or groups of people." It seems that prejudicial attitudes are quite well established, particularly among Whites who live in close proximity to American Indians. Unfortunately, once established, these prejudgments are difficult to eradicate and continue in the same or more virulent form from generation to generation.

Let me share two personal examples with you. In the spring of 1990, in a predominately White community that neighbors a midwestern reservation, a White clothing store owner who was renting tuxedos for the area junior proms was boycotted by the reservation high school. The reason was simple. After the merchant had gone to the reservation high school to take orders and measurements, he received a call from a man who wanted to secure a tuxedo for his son who had been absent on the day the merchant came to the high school. The merchant told the man that it would be no problem for his son to come in and get measured. It was at this point that the merchant asked him if he was White. The man, who was participating in a teacher exchange program with Massachusetts, replied yes. The merchant then stated that there was no need for him to put down the $35 deposit required from everyone else at the school because he was White. The merchant said, "We get deposits from the Indian people down there because we have had trouble with them in the past doing business. They have trouble handling money." Needless to say, when this was reported to the high school, the junior and senior classes voted unanimously to cancel their tuxedo orders from the merchant.[2]

Another revealing incident involved a colleague of mine who was living in New England. She was purchasing a birthday present for one of her son's friends. Because she is a strong advocate of nonviolence, when the store clerk took her over to the display of toy guns, she said she made a habit of not buying anything that encourages the use of violence, such as war toys. He then replied, "Well, how about this one? You don't have to tell him it is a war toy. You can just say that it is used for killing Indians and have them play cowboys and Indians."

In addition to these examples, racial slurs and slogans are everpresent in the lives of American Indians. Many I have talked with have been called such things as "wagon burners," "savages," and "prairie niggers," or have been told that "the only good Indian is a dead Indian." Almost any Indian youth will tell you exactly which stores he or she feels comfortable in and which stores he or she is not welcome in. This is the reality of racism for many American Indians.

To combat this racist reality, aggressive efforts must focus on implementing programs within communities and school systems that accurately educate the White population about the cultural heritage of American Indian people. If negative Indian stereotypes and racism are ever to be overcome, the White population's understanding and appreciation of American Indian culture and heritage are essential. While many believe that a deeply prejudiced person is almost immune to information such as this, it is important to begin with the new generation while they are still forming their attitudes about the world around them.

ECONOMIC BARRIERS

Of course, a significant reduction of prejudice and racism is perhaps more likely to occur if we change the structural conditions of poverty and inequality that promote these prejudicial attitudes. Indicators of poverty were consistently found to be related to the forms of violence studied in this book. To simply say, however, that American Indians experience economic deprivation is not enough to convey the magnitude of the problem. Unemployment on some reservations is as high as 90 percent. According to the 1980 Census, nearly one of every four American Indian families has an income that is below the poverty level (Snipp and Summers, 1991). While some gains were made during the "war on poverty" in the 1960s and 1970s, it appears that the 1980s have brought a downturn in the economic standing of most tribes. Many tribes are dependent on federal support for jobs and other assistance, so that the reductions in federal spending that occurred during the Reagan years sharply increased unemployment and poverty on many reservations.

The need for culturally sensitive economic development for those who live on reservations is an urgent one. By "culturally sensitive," I mean development that is consistent with most native values regarding the environment. All too often companies propose to bring jobs to Indian reservations, but only bring temporary employment and then leave behind such things as toxic waste and environmental degradation.[3]

LaDuke and Churchill (1985) term this process "radioactive colonialism." They describe several instances in which companies not only left Indian communities without jobs, but also left them with serious health threats. LaDuke and Churchill describe an incident that occurred between the Navajo Nation and Kerr-McGee Oil that should unquestionably illustrate the devastating effects I am talking about:

The Navajo Tribal council approved a mineral extraction agreement with Kerr-McGee in 1952. In return for access to uranium deposits near the town of Shiprock on the reservation, Kerr-McGee employed 100 Navajo men in underground mining operations.

Wages for these non-union Navajo miners were low, averaging $1.60 per hour or approximately two-thirds of the then-prevailing off-reservation rate. By 1969 . . . recoverable uranium deposits at Shiprock had been exhausted. Further, the Atomic Energy Commission was in the process of phasing out its ore-buying program. . . . The Shiprock facility was closed, for all practical purposes, in early 1970.

For the Navajo people, Kerr-McGee's abrupt departure shed light upon the "diseconomies" of uranium development. The corporation had simply abandoned at the site some 71 acres of "raw" uranium tailings, which retain 85% of the original radioactivity of the ore. This huge pile of tailings begins approximately sixty *feet* from the San Juan River, the only significant water source within the Shiprock area.

The price of Kerr-McGee's "development" at Shiprock cannot be calculated by any economic yardstick. Of the 150-odd Navajo miners who worked underground at the facility, eighteen had died of radiation-induced lung cancer by 1975. By 1980, twenty more were dead, and another ninety-five had contracted respiratory ailments and cancers. Birth defects such as cleft palate, leukemia and other diseases commonly linked to increased radiation exposure have risen dramatically both at Shiprock and in the downstream communities. (pp. 113-114)

In contrast to this horror story and to the generally bleak economic conditions under which many American Indians live, there are several examples of economic success that have not been denigrating to either the environment or the people. In fact, several tribes have generated astounding economic victories.[4] For example, the Warm Springs Confederation (which is composed of the Wascos, the Warm Springs, and the Paiutes from Oregon) is perhaps the largest employer in central Oregon. The Confederation owns and operates several businesses, including a hydroelectric plant, a timber and sawmill operation, a sewing plant, and a four-star resort. These, along with other smaller businesses, net the Confederation millions of dollars each year and provide hundreds of jobs.

The Passamaquoddies of Maine have also achieved remarkable economic success in the world of business. They own a large cement factory, the state's third largest commercial wild blueberry farm (which now provides blueberries exclusively to Ben and Jerry's Ice Cream), two radio stations, a supermarket, a mall and a forestry operation. When all these operations are combined, the tribe controls one of the state's largest private portfolios. Other examples of Indian economic self-sufficiency include the White Mountain Apaches of Arizona, who own the state's largest ski resort; the Swinomish of Washington, who are building a huge marina and restaurant along with a multimillion dollar hotel on Padilla Bay; and the Cherokee of North Carolina, who own Carolina Mirror, the largest mirror manufacturer in the United States. This honor role of successful tribes is by no means exhaustive, but should help illustrate the range of possibilities that can shift a tribe from a position of economic dependency to one of self-sufficiency under conditions of tribal sovereignty.

FAMILY INTERVENTIONS

The colonization process has produced other forms of dislocation among the American Indian people besides economic dislocation. This process has also created many unique pressures on the relationships among American Indian family members. As we have already seen in this book, indicators of social disorganization, such as divorce and other forms of family disruption, can foster such maladies as aggression directed toward others. When a community is living under conditions of extreme deprivation, it is not surprising that the stresses of everyday existence are played out in the family context.

The results of the research presented in this book, along with other research, suggest that families may be stress collection points not ony for stressful events created within the family, but also for stresses originating outside of the family.[5] People often express their anger and frustration toward family members in ways that would be unacceptable if used outside the family. This ventilation of frustrations within the family sometimes escalates from verbal confrontations to physical aggression, and a certain proportion of these situations become lethal. American Indian families must have resources available in order to become the backbone of American Indian communities that they once were. Programs that teach family members effective ways to communicate and also techniques to manage and reduce stress are seriously needed in most American Indian communities.

Further, research indicates that supportive human relationships can protect stressed individuals against a variety of ills. Therefore, programs that teach American Indian families how to build these supportive networks can have positive consequences on several levels. These social supports for individuals can provide increased reassurance of worth, increase self-concept and self-esteem, assist in problem solving, and help prevent demoralization in times of stress.

Because most of the violence examined in this book has been male-perpetrated (including a higher rate of suicide for males), these programs should aggressively seek male participants. Other literature further substantiates this need. For example, studies of coping mechanisms find that females show a greater propensity to mobilize social supports in times of stress. In addition, females are more likely than males to seek out social support, to receive social support, and to be pleased with the support they receive. There may be an additional stigma for American Indian males to perform emotively. These men must learn that seeking social supports does not threaten their competence or independence and that displaying emotions other than anger does not threaten their masculinity.

Of course, the goal of this recommendation is to restabilize American Indian families that may be in crisis. Against this ideal backdrop of restabilization, however, is the reality for many American Indians of a family life characterized by chaos and destructive modes of communication. When domestic situations become violent, family members who become the victims of this violence must have havens in which to seek shelter. Most Indian communities are in desperate need of such safe havens. Of immediate importance here is the funding of battered women's shelters to meet the needs of abused American Indian women and their children. When there is no alternative within a family but divorce or disruption, steps must also be taken to assure the best interests of any children who may be involved. American Indian child-welfare services need to become more aware of the deleterious effects that removing a child from both his culture and his family may have. When questions of custody arise, both Indian children and their parents should have the right to counsel and access to the services of expert witnesses. If removal of an Indian child is the only solution, foster and adoptive parents must be provided who have adequate means and knowledge to meet *both* the cultural and the structural needs of that child.

CULTURAL CHOICE

A majority of American Indians today live in a dual world in which they must balance the dictates of modern society and those of their cultural heritage. Chapter 3 discussed in detail the devastating consequences that this culture conflict can have on an individual's psyche. Programs must be implemented that promote self-esteem and self-worth by instilling a positive American Indian identity. In a letter to Senator Edward Kennedy, a young Indian woman writes:

I can't predict how I should educate my children, but one thing I know is, if my children are proud, if my children have identity, if my children know who they are and if they're proud to be who they are, they'll be able to encounter anything in life. I think this is what education means. Some people say that a man without education might as well be dead. I say, a man without identity—if a man doesn't know who he is—he might as well be dead.

Inconsistent policies imposed by the U.S. government have created a virtual wasteland as far as American Indian identities are concerned.[6] During the past 150 years, the policy of the U.S. government toward American Indians can be characterized as having five distinct periods: (1) *separation*, during which the prime objective was to remove Indians from the land that Whites desired and draw boundaries between the two peoples; (2) *coercive assimilation*, during which Whites sought to replace Indian culture with the dominant White culture and to help Indians become self-sufficient farmers and artisans, under conditions deemed suitable by Whites; (3) *tribal restoration, phase I*, during which Whites reversed previous policy and encouraged Indians to maintain their corporate tribal existence if they chose to do so; (4) *termination*, during which the objective was to break off all relationships of protection and assistance with the federal government; and (5) *tribal restoration, phase II*, during which tribal corporate adaptation to American society was again encouraged and cultural choice was reaffirmed.

This inconsistency has perhaps been one of the leading contributors to the culture conflict that many American Indians perceive today. Consistent policy is needed whereby every American Indian is given the opportunity to explore his or her heritage and culture. There are several ways to encourage this development. Aggressive educational efforts that encourage cultural choice must be implemented. Steps should be taken, for example, to include Indian languages in school textbooks, teach Indian languages in local Indian schools, and revive Indian religions.

The Native American Language Issues Institute believes that native languages are disappearing at a rate of five per year, with only 200 languages left alive. Shirley Brown, executor at the Institute, states, "We're always only one generation away from the loss of these very precious gifts" (*Rapid City Journal*, June 7, 1990, p. B3). Most agree that language is a very important reflection of culture and that its loss is a devastating blow to Indian heritage. Most older people I talked with on reservations across the country remember a time when they were punished for speaking in their native tongue. To prevent further decline, it is important that the rights of Indian people to preserve and promote their respective languages not be jeopardized again.

Programs that provide cultural education must be implemented both in the school systems and in communities to allow educational access to all. This access must be available not only to the Indian population, but to the general population as well. If negative Indian stereotypes and racism are ever to be overcome, the White population's understanding of American Indian culture and heritage is essential.

ALCOHOL AND DRUG USE

One of the most unequivocal findings of this book is that alcohol and drug use have a direct effect on both internal and external forms of violence. What is even more distressing is that the deleterious effects of alcohol abuse go far beyond those examined in this book. Alcohol abuse also causes premature death among American Indian populations in the form of accidents, cirrhosis of the liver, and alcohol psychosis.

The programs that have been implemented thus far to combat alcohol problems in American Indian populations have several limitations. For example, the Navajo Health Authority evaluated nine alcoholism programs designed for American Indians. The results of this evaluation project illuminated several major problems, including (1) extremely poor pay and no career ladder for counselors and other employees, (2) inadequate funding, (3) counselors with little or no professional training, (4) counseling that was generally limited to individual adult clients with little emphasis on family and community, (5) isolation from professional and community input, (6) neglect of the Indian spiritual aspects of life, (7) little follow-up, (8) a need for diversified staff and treatments, and (9) no guiding theoretical or ideological perspective. Other evaluation projects have revealed similar shortcomings.[7]

These points were corroborated by many people I interviewed. One counselor who worked at a battered women's shelter stated:

There are many people who would like to get treatment. There is a very long waiting list. So instead of doing intervention when someone has hit rock bottom, a lot of times you have got to be sober for months before you can get into treatment. This obviously rules out a lot of people. They try to treat the people who might make it the best instead of those who need the treatment the most. People who have money can get into treatment programs when they hit rock bottom. But no one has money here. Here it is not like that. It's like if you get your act together enough to go, then we will think about sending you—then maybe you can get on a waiting list.

The director of one intervention program also validated the inadequacies found by the Navajo project. He states, ''The quality of follow-up is no good, if it exists at all. And the turnover in counselors is incredible. They themselves are usually in and out of treatment. It takes time to get through the trauma of recovering yourself and sometimes they put those folks right into counseling positions right out of treatment. It is a bad situation.''

In perhaps the best review of alcohol and drug misuse prevention programs, May (1986) states:

Indian alcoholism programs have had a short but highly political and frustrating history. They have been low-budget, client-oriented counseling programs staffed exclusively by recovered Indian alcoholics. The services offered are usually limited to outpatient therapy for motivated clients. Only a few offer detoxication and a limited number offer some combination of residential treatment halfway houses and occupational opportunities. (p. 190)

In his review, May (1986) outlines three recommendations for improving alcohol and drug misuse programs. The first involves the establishment of programs that seek primary prevention by applying a public health approach to minimize alcohol and drug misuse, morbidity, and mortality among American Indians. "The goal should be to keep people alive and healthy during the youthful period of experimentation with alcohol and drugs so that they at least live to have a chance to adopt a nonabusive life style" (p. 190). May illustrates this approach by outlining strategies that would help to decrease alcohol-related automobile accidents, such as improved medical care, new legislation and enforcement for deterrence, improved road engineering, and mandatory passenger restraints.

A second type of program should provide Indian communities with specific and comprehensive information about drug and alcohol misuse and should direct such educational efforts at youth. May (1986) notes that there is all too often a fatalistic acceptance of alcohol problems that must be replaced by knowledge and "a positivistic orientation that may lessen some of their problems without being intrusive into their traditional way of life" (p. 192).

Finally, rehabilitation programs should provide a variety of therapies using both modern and traditional Indian approaches. Many Indians share different philosophies about the appropriate treatments. Some I talked with strongly advocate secular programs, such as Alcoholics Anonymous, while others hold that the traditional or "red road" approach (i.e., religious treatments, such as sweatbaths ceremonies, and so forth) is the most appropriate treatment. Program strategies will be most beneficial if they offer these approaches in combination, rather than juxtaposed as opposing methods of therapy. May (1986) summarizes these policy recommendations best: "the goal of any rehabilitation program should be to help the individual regain new sources of positive integration with relatives, and new coping skills for both modern and traditional cultures" (p. 193).

CONCLUSION

This research has perhaps generated many more questions than it has actually answered. Future research should test the theories advanced in this book on a tribal-specific basis. There is also a need to explore the differences that exist in the etiology of violence between rural and urban Indian populations. Many other questions need to be addressed. For example, do tribes that have become economically self-sufficient have lower rates of violence than do tribes with higher rates of poverty? What contemporary cultural elements exist within tribal communities that lead to a higher propensity for outward- rather than inward-directed violence?

Too often we think that we are powerless to change situations and circumstances for ourselves or for those around us. But organizations and concerned individuals do bring about change. For the reader's information, Appendix B provides a list of organizations and alliances that are working toward some of the same goals that have been described in this chapter.

It is hoped that the conclusions drawn from this research will go on to be refined by future work and that this work will be a catalyst for future empirical investigations. There is still so much to be understood. As the quotation that began this book so eloquently states:

People are just beginning to understand the problems. We can't answer it for ourselves as a tribe. We need outside people to help us. That work is going to bridge our world with yours, our way of thinking with your way of thinking and we need that bridge. It's like a puzzle. And there's many pieces to that puzzle and they all can connect to each other. It's just that you need people with intelligence to say "Hey, let's put the puzzle down on the table and let's connect these pieces together. And let's build a story. And let's let the whole world hear that story. And it's a puzzle—a puzzle about people.

NOTES

1. For detailed account of Chippewa account, see *The Progressive*, April 1990, pp. 20-23.

2. For account of this incident see *The Rapid City Journal*, May 5, 1990.

3. There are many instances of things like this happening to tribes around the country. For example, the Peabody Coal Company convinced two Arizona tribal councils in 1966 to sign thirty-five-year leases, allowing them to mine over 3,000 square miles of land for uranium, oil, and other minerals. Elsewhere, the Honeywell Company is constructing a munitions test facility in a remote canyon that is a traditional religious ceremonial area for the Sioux Indians.

4. For detailed case studies of some of these tribal success, see White, 1990.

5. See Bachman, Linsky, and Straus, 1988.

6. Many authors have given detailed discussion of this inconsistent policy including Deloria, 1988, 1985b; and Harvard Encyclopedia of American Ethnic Groups, 1980.

7. See the Navajo Health Authority, 1979 and Raymond & Raymond, 1984.

Interview Questionnaire

Informed Consent Form

The purpose of this research is to understand what it is like to grow up an as American Indian in this country. I also hope to gain insight into your perception of the crime that you were convicted of and about your attitudes about violence in general. Because most people know very little about the lives and attitudes of American Indians today, I also hope that you can tell me your views and attitudes about your life and about the lives of your people. Participation in this interview is completely voluntary - you will receive no rewards for your participation. You are also free to withdraw your participation at any time during the interview.

These interviews are for my own research at the University of New Hampshire and are in NO WAY connected with the prison, the government, or any other federal agency. Although the information received from these interviews will be held strictly confidential and used for my own analysis only, you must know that any information you give me can be subpoenaed in court and in order to protect yourself from this, do not give me any information that could possibly incriminate you on other charges. As I am asking for your permission to tape record these interviews, I want you to know that these tapes will be destroyed as soon as they are transcribed on paper which will be no later than six weeks from the date of our interview.

I certify that I have read and fully understand the purpose of this research project and its risks and benefits for me as stated above.

Signature of respondent _____

Date _____

Questionnaire

Part I. Introduction

A1. Where did you grow up?

A2. What was it like for you growing up?

A3. Is there anything else?

A4. What issues about crime in the United States are of the most concern
    to you?

Part II. I would like to hear your opinions and views about a number of
issues, especially crime in America and about violence in general.

B1. I'd like you to tell me how wrong you think the men involved in the
following situations are by answering on a scale from zero to ten. Zero means
you think the man is not wrong at all and ten means you think he is extremely
wrong. You can use any number between zero and ten to indicate how wrong the
man's hitting is in each situation (Hand respondent response card). You are
welcome to elaborate on your response at any time.

    How wrong would it be for a stranger to hit a man...
B2. Who was in a protest march showing opposition to
    the other man's views?

    0   1   2   3   4   5   6   7   8   9   10
B3. Who was drunk and bumped into the other man and his wife on the street?

    0   1   2   3   4   5   6   7   8   9   10
B4. Who had hit another man's child after the child had accidently damaged
    his car?

    0   1   2   3   4   5   6   7   8   9   10
B5. Who was beating up a woman and the other man saw it?

    0   1   2   3   4   5   6   7   8   9   10
B6. Who had broken into another man's house?

    0   1   2   3   4   5   6   7   8   9   10
B7. Who had said something to insult another man?

    0   1   2   3   4   5   6   7   8   9   10

B8. Are there any other situations that you might feel it appropriate for a
    man to hit another man?

Part III. Here are some things people often say about violence in our society. I would like to know whether you Strongly Agree, Agree, Disagree, or Strongly Disagree (Give respondent scale and probe for elaboration of answers at the end of each statement).

D1. Violence deserves violence.

D2. It's important to be kind to people even if they do things you don't believe in.

D3. An eye for an eye and a tooth for a tooth is a good rule for living.

D4. It is often necessary to use violence to prevent violence.

D5. When a person harms you, you should turn the other cheek and forgive him.

D6. When someone does wrong, he should be paid back for it.

D7. Many people only learn through violence.

D8. Even if you don't like a person, you should still try to help him.

D9. A man has a right to kill another man in a case of self defense.

D10. A man has the right to kill a person to defend his family.

D11. A man has the right to kill a person to defend his house.

D12. Even if it means giving up something, you should help others get what they want.

D13. People who make speeches stirring people up should be put in prison before they cause serious trouble.

D14. Police are getting so much power the average citizen has to worry.

D15. Courts nowadays are much too easy on criminals.

D16. Protest in which some people are hurt is necessary for changes to come fast enough.

D17. How many of your friends do you think would agree with your answers?

Part IV.

E1. When people get into fights, even if those fights end up with someone getting killed, there are different reasons for the fights happening. Thinking about it generally, I would like you to think about what some of the causes might be. For each reason I mention, I would like you to tell me how often you think it applies - never, sometimes, or most of the time - and why.

E2. Do you think poverty causes violence?

E3. Do you think unemployment causes violence?

E4. Do alcohol or drugs contribute to violence?

E5. Does discrimination cause violence?

E6. Does feeling unimportant cause violence?

E7. Does violence occur because a guy feels put down?

E8. Does violence happen because a person sees no other way of solving a
   problem?

E9. Are there any other causes of violence that you can think of?

Part V.   Now I'd like to ask you some questions about different kinds of
crime.

F1. Some people say that stealing or damaging property is as bad as hurting
people. Others say that damaging property is not as bad as hurting people.
What do you think?

F2. For the following crimes, I would like you to tell me how serious you
think each crime is based on scale from one to nine with one being least
serious and nine being most serious.

	Least Serious								Most Serious
Selling drugs	1	2	3	4	5	6	7	8	9
Driving while drunk	1	2	3	4	5	6	7	8	9
Planned killing of a cop	1	2	3	4	5	6	7	8	9
Forcible rape	1	2	3	4	5	6	7	8	9
Stealing from a business	1	2	3	4	5	6	7	8	9
Killing someone in a fight	1	2	3	4	5	6	7	8	9
Armed robbery of a business	1	2	3	4	5	6	7	8	9
Spying for a foreign government	1	2	3	4	5	6	7	8	9
Causing the death of someone	1	2	3	4	5	6	7	8	9
because of drunk driving	1	2	3	4	5	6	7	8	9
Deserting the enemy in time	1	2	3	4	5	6	7	8	9
of war	1	2	3	4	5	6	7	8	9
Impulsive killing of a spouse	1	2	3	4	5	6	7	8	9
Refusal to pay parking fines	1	2	3	4	5	6	7	8	9
Parent to child incest	1	2	3	4	5	6	7	8	9

Being drunk in public places   1 2 3 4 5 6 7 8 9

Shoplifting from a store   1 2 3 4 5 6 7 8 9

Theft of a car   1 2 3 4 5 6 7 8 9

Beating up a child   1 2 3 4 5 6 7 8 9

Deliberately starting a fire   1 2 3 4 5 6 7 8 9

Skipping school   1 2 3 4 5 6 7 8 9

Beating up an acquaintance   1 2 3 4 5 6 7 8 9

Disturbing the peace   1 2 3 4 5 6 7 8 9

Using drugs   1 2 3 4 5 6 7 8 9

Beating up a spouse   1 2 3 4 5 6 7 8 9

Selling liquor to minors   1 2 3 4 5 6 7 8 9

F3. How do you think robbery and stealing could be reduced?

    Any other ways?

    Which way is the best?

F4. How do you think murder rates could be reduced?

    Any other ways?

    Which way is the best?

F5. Do you think that all people are treated fairly in the courts today?

F6. How are they not treated fairly or equally?

F7. Do you think that the courts treat people like yourself (American Indian) better or worse than others?

F8. On the whole, would you say that the police are trying to be helpful or that they are looking for trouble?

F9. Do you think they treat people like yourself fairly?

Part VI. If it's okay with you, I'd like to ask you some specific questions about the crime that you were sent here for. Do you think your conviction was fair?

What were the events that led up to your conviction?

What were you thinking about and how did you feel just before it happened?

After it happened?

Were you drinking or using drugs?

Do you feel that the act was justified? Why or why not?

How do you feel about it now?

How does your family feel about it?

How do your friends feel about it?

What do you think caused it?

Do you think that it could have been prevented? (IF YOU DON'T KNOW THE WEAPON

INVOLVED AT THIS TIME, ASK)

How long have you been in prison?

Do you have any goals set for yourself when you get out of here?

Do you think you can achieve them? How?

Part VII.

C1. Now I'd like to ask you some questions about your social activities with people close to you. At the time the crime occurred...

	How many times per month did you...?	How important was that to you?
		NI SI VI EI
C2. Get together socially with relatives	0 1 2 3-5 5+	1 2 3 4
C3. Get together socially with friends	0 1 2 3-5 5+	1 2 3 4
C4. Do something special with spouse/girlfriend	0 1 2 3-5 5+	1 2 3 4
C5. Attend religious services or other religious activities	0 1 2 3-5 5+	1 2 3 4

Part VIII. Do any of these people keep in touch with you now? How so?

C6. How often does your family visit you now?	0 1 2 3-5 5+	1 2 3 4
Friends?	0 1 2 3-5 5+	1 2 3 4
Partner/Spouse?	0 1 2 3-5 5+	1 2 3 4
C7. How often do you get letters or calls from family?	0 1 2 3-5 5+	1 2 3 4
Friends?	0 1 2 3-5 5+	1 2 3 4
Partner/Spouse?	0 1 2 3-5 5+	1 2 3 4

C8. When you get out of here, what do you think your relationship with your family will be like?

With your friends?

With your partner/spouse?

Part IX. Now I'd like to ask you about your physical well-being. In the past year, how often have you...(read item and hand respondent response card)

	Never	Almost Never	Some- times	Fairly Often	Very Often
Had headaches or pains in the head	0	1	2	3	4
Been bothered by cold sweats	0	1	2	3	4
Felt nervous or stressed	0	1	2	3	4
Been bothered by feelings of sadness or depression	0	1	2	3	4
Felt difficulties were piling up so high that you could not overcome them	0	1	2	3	4
Felt very bad or worthless	0	1	2	3	4
Found that you could not cope with all of the things you had to do	0	1	2	3	4
Had times when you couldn't help wondering if anything was worthwhile anymore	0	1	2	3	4
Felt completely hopeless about everything	0	1	2	3	4
Been afraid to leave your cell	0	1	2	3	4
Thought about taking your own life	0	1	2	3	4

Now I'd like to finish up with a few background questions.

Are your parents alive?

When you were growing up, about how often, if ever, would you say your father used physical punishment? (spanking, slapping)
Your mother?

When you were growing up, about how often, if ever, did your mother and father get into physical fights?

Did they ever hit each other?

What does your father do for a living?

Did you ever have any desire to go further? If so, what prevented you?

Would you call yourself a religious person?

What type of religion would you classify yourself as?

How often do you attend religious services?

Were you religious when you were growing up?

Were you ever in any of the armed services?
If yes, did you ever have combat duty? During a war?
How do you feel about this experience?

What is the one thing that you would like people to know about you?

I thank you very much for your time and help.

Indian Affairs Organizations

AMERICAN INDIAN CULTURE RESEARCH CENTER
P.O. Box 98
Blue Cloud Abbey
Marvin, SD 57521
Corporation that supports Indian leaders and Indian educators in rebuilding the Indian community. Aids in teaching the non-Indian public about the culture and philosophy of the Indian. Serves as a resource for guidance and funding in Indian self-help programs.
Publications: Distributes films, books, records, and tapes.

AMERICAN INDIAN HERITAGE FOUNDATION
6051 Arlington Boulevard
Falls Church, VA 22044
Purpose is to inform and educate non-Indians concerning the culture and heritage of the American Indian. Seeks to inspire Indian youth.
Publications: Pathfinder Newsletter (quarterly); *Project Letter* (monthly); *Tsa-La-Gi Columns* (quarterly); brochures.

AMERICAN INDIAN MOVEMENT
710 Clayton Street, Apt. 1
San Francisco, CA 94117
Primary objectives are to encourage self-determination among American Indians and to establish international recognition of American Indian treaty rights.
Publication: Survival News (quarterly).

AMERICANS FOR INDIAN OPPORTUNITY
3508 Garfield Street, NW
Washington, DC 20007
Promotes economic self-sufficiency for American Indian tribes and individuals, and political self-government for members of American Indian tribes. Seeks to

help American Indians establish self-help programs at the local level, improve communications among Native Americans and with non-Indians, educate the public on the achievements and current needs of Native Americans. Supports projects in education, health, housing, job development, and job training for Indian youth. Assists in establishing local centers with similar goals.

Publications: Red Alert (periodic); *You Don't Have to Be Poor to Be Indian* (resource information).

ARROW, INCORPORATED

1000 Connecticut Avenue, NW, Suite 401
Washington, DC 20036

ARROW stands for Americans for Restitution and Righting of Old Wrongs. Dedicated to the advancement of the American Indian. Seeks to help the American Indian achieve better educational, cultural, and economic standards. Works to improve tribal law and justice.

Publications: American Indian Courtline (periodic); *Americans for Restitution and Righting of Old Wrongs* (annual); *Protecting Youth from Alcohol and Substance Abuse: What Can We Do?* (handbook).

CONCERNED AMERICAN INDIAN PARENTS

Cuhcc Clinic
22016 16th Avenue, South
Minneapolis, MN 55430

Serves as a network for American Indian parents and others interested in abolishing symbols that are degrading to American Indians. Seeks to make the future easier for American Indian children by educating the public about the racial messages inherent in such symbols.

DAKOTA WOMEN OF ALL RED NATIONS

c/o Lorelei DeCora
P.O. Box 423
Rosebud, SD 57570

Organization of American Indian women seeking to advance the Native American movement by establishing local chapters to work on issues of concern, such as community education, legal and juvenile justice problems, and problems caused by energy resource development by multinational corporations on Indian land.

INDIAN LAW RESOURCE CENTER

6021 East Street, SE
Washington, DC 20003

A legal, educational, counseling, and research service for American Indians and other Indians in the Western Hemisphere. Seeks to enable Indian peoples to survive as distinct peoples with unique cultures and to combat discrimination and injustice in the law and in public policy.

Publications: Indian Rights—Human Rights (handbook), articles, reports, and reprints.

INDIAN RIGHTS ASSOCIATION

c/o Janey Montgomery
1601 Market Street

Philadelphia, PA 19103
Aims to protect the legal and human rights of American Indians. Maintains first-hand knowledge of conditions in Indian communities, keeps in touch with governmental Indian affairs, and reports on judicial and legislative activities involving Indian concerns.
Publication: Indian Truth (bimonthly).

INDIAN YOUTH OF AMERICA
609 Badgerow Building
P.O. Box 2786
Sioux City, IA 51106
Dedicated to improving the lives of Indian children. Works to provide opportunities and experiences that will aid Indian youth in their educational, career, cultural, and personal growth. Goals of the program: to inform families, social service agencies, and courts about the rights of Indian people under the Indian Child Welfare Act; to counsel Indian children and their parents and recruit Indian foster homes for Indian children.
Publication: Indian Youth of America—Newsletter (quarterly).

INSTITUTE FOR THE DEVELOPMENT OF INDIAN LAW
c/o K. Kirke Kickingbird
Oklahoma City University
School of Law
2501 North Blackwelder
Oklahoma City, OK 73106
Special emphasis on Indian sovereignty, encouragement of Indian self-confidence and self-government, clarification of historical and legal foundations of modern Indian rights.
Publications: American Indian Journal (quarterly); *The Indians and the U.S. Constitution* (book, brochure, and videotape).

NATIONAL CONGRESS OF AMERICAN INDIANS
900 Pennsylvania Avenue, SE
Washington, DC 20003
Seeks to protect, conserve, and develop Indian natural and human resources; improve health, education, and economic conditions.
Publication: Annual Conference Report, Sentinel (periodic).

NATIONAL INDIAN SOCIAL WORKERS ASSOCIATION
P.O. Box 1667
Albuquerque, NM 87103
Advocates the rights of American Indians and Alaska Natives in social services areas. Provides counseling, program development, and planning and administration training and assistance to tribal and nontribal organizations.
Publications: National Indian Social Workers Association—The Association (periodic).

NATIONAL INDIAN YOUTH COUNCIL
318 Elm Street, SE
Albuquerque, NM 87102
Provides young Indian people with the working knowledge needed to serve and understand their tribal communities and develops educational resources through

research, training, and planning on local, regional, and national levels. Concerns include protecting Indian natural resources, tribal and individual civil liberties, and all matters related to the preservation of the Indian family unit and community.

Publications: Americans Before Columbus (bimonthly); *Indian Elected Officials Directory* (biennial); *Indian Voter Survey Reports* (periodic).

NATIVE AMERICAN COMMUNITY BOARD
2838 W. Peterson
Chicago, IL 60659
Works for the educational, social, and economic advancement of American Indians. Maintains Native American Women Health Education Resource Center, which provides self-help programs and workshops on such issues as family planning, fetal alcohol syndrome, domestic abuse and crisis, and child development. Offers support services to Native Americans seeking employment and educational opportunities.

Publications: Wicozanni-Wowapi (quarterly); brochures and pamphlets.

NATIVE AMERICAN RIGHTS FUND
1506 Broadway
Boulder, CO 80302
Represents Indian individuals and tribes in legal matters of national significance. Areas of concern are tribal existence; protection of tribal resources; human rights, including educational matters and religious freedom; accountability of federal, state, and tribal governments; Indian law development.

Publication: Indian Law Support Center Reporter (monthly newsletter).

NORTH AMERICAN INDIAN WOMEN'S ASSOCIATION
P.O. Box 805
Eagle Butte, SD 57625
Seeks to foster through unity of purpose the general well-being of Indian people. Promotes intertribal communication; awareness of Native American culture; betterment of family life, health, and education; and strengthened communication among Native Americans.

Publication: Brochure.

SURVIVAL OF AMERICAN INDIANS ASSOCIATION
7803-A Samurai Drive, SE
Olympia, WA 98503
Provides public education on Indian rights and tribal reform action. Supports independent Indian education institutions.

Publication: The Renegade: A Strategy Journal of Indian Opinion (periodic).

UNITED INDIANS OF ALL TRIBES FOUNDATION
Daybreak Star Arts Center
Discovery Park
P.O. Box 99100
Seattle, WA 98199
Promotes the interests of Native Americans. Helps to develop and expand Native American economic self-sufficiency, education, and arts. Affiliated with National

Congress of American Indians.
Publication: Daybreak Star (monthly magazine).

UNITED NATIVE AMERICANS
2434 Faria Avenue
Pinole, CA 94564
Purposes are to promote the general welfare of Native Americans; to provide legal aid, housing, food, lodging, and counseling.
Publication: Warpath (monthly).

Bibliography

Aase, J. M. (1981). The fetal alcohol syndrome in American Indians: A high risk group. *Neurobehavioral Toxicology & Teratology, 3,* 153-156.

Akers, R. L. (1985). *Deviant behavior: A social learning approach* (3rd ed.). Belmont, CA: Wadsworth Publishing Co.

Aldrich, J. H. & Nelson, F. D. (1984). *Linear probability, logit, and probit models.* Newbury Park, CA: Sage Publications.

Annals of America (Vol. 1). Encyclopaedia Britannica.

Archer, D. (1983). *Violence and culture: Differences and similarities across different cultures.* Unpublished manuscript.

Bachman, R. (1991). The social causes of American Indian homicide as revealed by the life expectancy of thirty offenders. *American Indian Quarterly, 15*(4), 469-92.

Bachman, R. (1991, November). An analysis of American Indian homicide: A test of social disorganization and economic deprivation at the reservation county level. *Journal of Research on Crime and Delinquency,* 76-84.

Bachman, R., Linsky, A. S., & Straus, M. A. (1988). *Homicide of family members, acquaintances, and strangers, and state-to-state differences in social stress, social control and social norms.* Paper presented at the meeting of the American Sociological Association, Atlanta, GA.

Badwound, E., & Tierney, W. G. (1988, October). Leadership and American Indian values: The tribal college dilemma. *Journal of American Indian Education,* 9-15.

Baker, J. L. (1959). Indians, alcohol and homicide. *Journal of Social Therapy, 5,* 270-275.

Baker, S. (1985). *Injury in America: A Continuing Public Health Problem.* Washington, DC: National Academy Press.

Baron, L., & Straus, M. A. (1989). *Four Theories of Rape in American Society: A State Level Analysis.* New Haven, CT: Yale University Press.

Beauvais, F., Oetting, E. R., & Edwards, R. W. (1985). Trends in the use of inhalants among American Indian adolescents. *White Cloud Journal, 3*(4), 3-11.

Beiser, M. (1972). Etiology of mental disorders: Sociocultural aspects. In B. Wold-man (Ed.), *Manual of child psychopathology*. New York: McGraw-Hill.

Beiser, M. (1981). Mental health of American Indian and Alaska Native children: Some epidemiologic perspectives. *White Cloud Journal, 2*(2), 37-47.

Berk, R. A. (1983). An introduction to sample selection bias. *American Sociological Review, 48*(3), 386-398.

Berlin, I. N. (1978). Anglo adoption of Native-Americans: Repercussions in adolescence. *Journal of the American Academy of Child Psychiatry, 17*(2), 387-388.

_____. (1982). Prevention of emotional problems among Native-American children: Overview of developmental issues. *Journal of Preventative Psychiatry, 1*(3), 319-330.

_____. (1986). Psychopathology and its antecedents among American Indian adolescents. In B. L. Lahey & I. N. Kazdin (Eds.), *Advances in clinical child psychology*. New York: Plenum.

_____. (1987). Suicide among American Indian adolescents: An overview. *Suicide & Life-Threatening Behavior, 17*(3), 218-232.

Bienvenue, R. M., & Latif, A. H. (1975). Arrests, disposition, and recidivism: A comparison of Indians and Whites. *Canadian Journal of Criminology & Corrections, 16*(2), 1-12.

Black, D. (1976). *The behavior of law*. New York: Academic Press.

Blanchard, J. D., Blanchard, E. L. & Rolls, R. (1986). Psychological autopsy of an Indian adolescent suicide with implications for community services. *Suicide & Life-Threatening Behavior, 6*, 3-10.

Blau, J. R., & Blau, P. M. (1982). The cost of inequality: Metropolitan structure and violent crime. *American Sociological Review, 47*, 114-129.

Blau, P. M., & Golden, R. M. (1986). Metropolitan structure and criminal violence. *Sociological Quarterly, 27*(1), 15-26.

Blauner, R. (1972). *Racial Oppression in America*. Chicago, IL: University of Chicago Press.

Blumer, H. (1969). *Symbolic interactionism*. Englewood Cliffs, NJ: Prentice-Hall.

Braithwaite, J. (1979). *Inequality, crime, and public policy*. London: Routledge & Kegan Paul.

Brenner, H. (1973). *Mental illness and the economy*. Cambridge, MA: Harvard University Press.

Broudy, D. W., & May, P. A. (1983). Demographic and epidemiologic transition among the Navajo Indians. *Social Biology, 30*(1), 1-16.

Brown, D. (1970). *Bury my heart at Wounded Knee*. New York: Washington Square Press.

Browne, A., & Williams, K. R. (1989). Exploring the effect of resource availability and the likelihood of female-perpetrated homicides. *Law and Society Review, 23*(1), 75-92.

Bruneau, O. J. (1984). Comparison of behavioral characteristics and self-concepts of American Indian and Caucasian preschoolers. *Psychological Reports, 54*, 571-574.

Bryde, J. D. (1970). *The Indian student: A study of scholastic failure and personality conflict*. Vermillion: University of South Dakota Press.

Byler, W. (1977). The destruction of American Indian families. In S. Unger (Ed.), *The destruction of the American Indian family*. New York: Association on American Indian Affairs.

Campbell, D. T., & Fiske, D. W. (1959). Convergent and discriminant validity by the multi-trait, multi-method matrix. *Psychological Bulletin, 56,* 126-139.

Cantor, D., & Land, K. C. (1985). Unemployment and crime rates in the post–World War II United States: A theoretical and empirical analysis. *American Sociological Review, 44,* 588-608.

Carlson, G. A., & Cantwell, D. P. (1982). Suicidal behavior and depression in children and adolescents. *Journal of the American Academy of Child Psychiatry, 21*(4), 361-368.

Chadwick, B. A., Strauss, J., Bahr, H. M., & Halverson, L. K. (1976). Confrontation with the law: The case of American Indians in Seattle. *Phylon, 37,* 163-171.

Chambliss, W. J., & Seidman, R. B. (1971). *Law, order, and power.* Reading, MA: Addison-Wesley Publishing Co.

Chiricos, T. G., Jackson, P. D., & Waldo, G. P. (1972). Inequality in the imposition of a criminal label. *Social Problems, 19,* 553-572.

Chiricos, T. G., & Waldo, G. P. (1975). Socioeconomic status and criminal sentencing. *American Sociological Review, 40,* 753-772.

Clinard, M. B. (1964). The theoretical implications of anomie and deviant behavior. In M. B. Clinard (Ed.), *Anomie and deviant behavior.* New York: Free Press.

Cloward, R. A., & Ohlin, L. E. (1960). *Delinquency and opportunity: A theory of delinquent gangs.* New York: Free Press.

Cockernam, W. C. (1975). Drinking attitudes and practices among Wind River Reservation youth. *Quarterly Journal of Studies on Alcohol, 36,* 321-326.

Cockernam, W. C., & Forslund, M. A. (1975). Attitudes toward the police among White and Indian Native American youth. *American Indian Law Review, 3*(2), 419-428.

Cohen, L. E., & Felson, M. (1979). Social change and crime rate trends: A routine activities approach. *American Sociological Review, 44,* 588-608.

Coladarci, T. (1983). High school dropout rate among Native Americans. *Journal of American Indian Education, 23*(4), 15-22.

Coleman, D. H. & Straus, M. A. (1983). Alcohol abuse and family violence. In E. Gottheil, K. A. Druley, T. E. Skolada, & H. M. Waxman (Eds.), *Alcohol, drug abuse and aggression.* Springfield, IL: Charles C. Thomas.

Cook, P. (1975). The correctional carrot: Better jobs for parolees. *Policy Analysis, 1*(2), 11-54.

Cook, P. J., & Zarkin, G. A. (1983). *Homicide and business conditions: A replication of H. Brenner's New Report to the U.S. Congress.* Mimeo. (Duke University, Durham, NC.)

————. (1985). *Homicide and economic conditions: A replication of H. Brenner's New Report to the U.S. Congress.* Mimeo. (Duke University, Durham, NC.)

Crutchfield, R. D., Geerken, M. R., & Gove, W. R. (1982). Crime rate and social integration. *Criminology, 20,* 467-478.

Curlee, W. V. (1969). Suicide and self-destructive behavior on the Cheyenne River Reservation. In *Suicide among the American Indians.* Rockville, MD: National Institute of Mental Health.

Curtis, L. A. (1975). *Violence, race, and culture.* Lexington, MA: Lexington Books.

Davenport, J. A., & Davenport, J. I. (1987). Native American suicide: A Durkheim analysis. *Social Casework, 68*(9), 535-539.

DeFronzo, J. (1983). Economic assistance to impoverished Americans: Relationship to incidence of crime. *Criminology, 21,* 119-136.

Deloria, V. (1985). *Behind the trail of broken treaties.* Austin: University of Texas Press.

Deloria, V. (1988). *Custer died for your sins.* Norman, OK: University of Oklahoma Press.

Denzin, N. K. (1970). *The research act in sociology.* London: Butterworth.

Deykin, E. Y., Alpert, J., & McNamara, J. J. (1985). A pilot study of the effect of child abuse or neglect on adolescent suicide behavior. *American Journal of Psychiatry, 142*(11), 1299-1303.

Devereux, G. (1942). Primitive psychiatry II: Funeral suicide and the Mohave social structure. *Bulletin of the History of Medicine, 11*(5), 522-542.

Dizmang, L. H., Watson, J., May, P. A., & Bopp, J. (1974). Adolescent suicide at an Indian reservation. *American Journal of Orthopsychiatry, 44*(1), 43-49.

Doerner, W. G. (1983). Why does Johny Reb die when shot? The impact of medical resources upon lethality. *Sociological Inquiry, 53,* 1-15.

Doerner, W. G., & Speir, J. C. (1986). Stitch and sew: The impact of medical resources upon criminally induced lethality. *Criminology, 24*(2), 319-330.

Durkheim, E. ([1897] 1951). *Suicide: A study in sociology.* Glencoe, IL: Free Press.

Farlow, B. A. (1979). *An equal chance: Handbook for counseling Indian students.* Unpublished report.

Farrington, K. (1980). Stress and family violence. In M. A. Straus & G. T. Hotaling (Eds.), *The social causes of husband-wife violence,* Minneapolis, MN: University of Minnesota Press.

Fenton, W. N. (1941). *Iroquois suicide: A study in the stability of a culture pattern.* Smithsonian Institution Bureau of American Ethnology Bulletin No. 128, Anthropological Papers No. 14. Washington, DC: U.S. Government Printing Office, 79-138.

Ferguson, F. N. (1968). Navajo drinking, some tentative hypotheses. *Human Organization, 27*(2), 159-167.

Fielding, N. G., & Fielding, J. L. (1986). *Linking data.* Beverly Hills, CA: Sage.

Fischer, C. S. (1975). Toward a subcultural theory of urbanism. *American Journal of Sociology, 80*(6), 1319-1341.

Fischler, R. S. (1985). Child abuse and neglect in American Indian communities. *Child Abuse & Neglect, 9,* 95-106.

Fisher, A. D. (1987). Alcoholism and race: The misapplication of both concepts to North American Indians. *Canadian Review of Sociology & Anthropology, 24*(1), 81-88.

Forslund, M. A., & Cranston, V. A. (1975). A self-report comparison of Indian and Anglo delinquency in Wyoming. *Criminology, 13*(2), 193-198.

Forslund, M. A., & Meyers, R. E. (1974). Delinquency among Wind River Indian Reservation youth. *Criminology, 12*(1), 197-205.

Fox, J. D., & Ward, J. A. (1984). An Indian community with a high suicide rate— Five years after. *Canadian Journal of Psychology, 29,* 425-427.

Frederick, C. J. (1973). *Suicide, homicide and alcoholism among American Indians: Guidelines for help.* Rockville, MD: National Institute of Mental Health.

French, L. (1980). An analysis of contemporary Indian justice and correctional treatment. *Federal Probation, 44*(3), 19-23.

French, L., & Hornbuckle, J. (1977). An analysis of Indian violence: The Cherokee example. *American Indian Quarterly, 3*(4), 335-356.

Frost-Reed, B. J., & May, P. A. (1984). Inhalant abuse and juvenile delinquency: A control study in Albuquerque, New Mexico. *International Journal of the Addictions, 19,* 789-803.

Fuchs, E., & Havighurst, R. J. (1970). *The self-esteem of American Indian youth: The personal/social adjustment of American Indian youth* (National Study of American Indian Series, Final Rep.). Chicago: University of Chicago Press.

Gabarino, J., & Ebata, A. (1983). The significance of ethnic and cultural differences in child maltreatment. *Journal of Marriage and the Family, 45,* 773-783.

Gastil, R. P. (1971). Homicide and regional culture of violence. *American Sociological Review, 36,* 412-427.

Gelles, R. J. (1974). *The violent home: A Study of physical aggression between husbands and wives.* Newbury Park, CA: Sage Publications.

Giovacchi, P. (1981). *The urge to die: Why young people commit suicide.* New York: Macmillan.

Glasser, D. (1982). *The effectiveness of a prison and parole system.* Indianapolis: Bobbs-Merril.

Gold, M. (1958). Suicide, homicide, and the socialization of aggression. *American Journal of Sociology, 63,* 651-661.

Gore, S. (1978). The effects of social support in moderating the health consequences of unemployment. *Journal of Health & Social Behavior, 19,* 157-165.

Graves, T. D. (1970). The personal adjustment of Navajo Indian migrants to Denver, Colorado. *American Anthropologist, 72*(1), 35-54.

Green, B. E., Sack, W. H., & Pambrun, A. (1981). A review of child psychiatric epidemiology with special reference to American Indian and Alaska Native children. *White Cloud Journal, 2*(2), 23-36.

Green, D. E. (1988). *Methodological issues in the study of Native American criminality.* Paper presented at the annual meeting of the American Society of Criminology, Montreal.

Green, H. J. (1983). Risks and attitudes with extra-cultural placement of American Indian children: A critical review. *Journal of the American Academy of Child Psychiatry,22*(1), 63-67.

Gundlach, J. H., & Roberts, A. E. (1978). Native American Indian migration and relocation: Success or failure. *Pacific Sociological Review, 21*(1), 117-128.

Hackney, S. (1969). Southern violence. In H. D. Graham & T. R. Gurr (Eds.), *Violence in America.* New York: Signet.

Hagan, J. (1976). Locking up the Indians: A case for law reform. *Canadian Forum, 55*(2), 16-18.

Hall, E., & Simkus, A. A. (1975). Inequality in the types of sentences received by Native Americans and Whites. *Criminology, 13,* 199-222.

Hanson, J. R., & Rouse, L. P. (1987). Dimensions of Native American stereotyping. *American Indian Culture & Research Journal, 11*(4), 22-30.

Hanson, J. R. & Rouse, L. P. (1990). *Racial and ethnic stereotyping: Facts, feelings, and followings.* Paper presented at the meeting of the American Sociologists Association, Washington, DC.

Hanushek, E. A., & Jackson, J. E. (1977). *Statistical methods for social scientists.* New York: Academic Press.

Haraldson, S.S.R. (1988). Health and health services among the Navajo Indians. *Journal of Community Health, 13*(3), 129-142.

Harries, K. D. (1985). The historical geography of homicide in the U.S., 1935-1980. *Geoforum, 16*(2), 73-83.

Hartwig, F., & Dearing, B. (1979). *Exploratory data analysis.*Beverly Hills, CA: Sage.

Harvard Encyclopedia of American Ethnic Groups. (1980). Cambridge, MA: Belknap Press.

Hawkins, D. F. (1983). Black and White homicide differentials: Alternatives to an inadequate theory. *Criminal Justice & Behavior, 10*(2), 407-440.

Hawkins, D. F. (1985). Black homicide: The adequacy of existing research for devising prevention strategies. *Crime & Delinquency, 31*(1), 83-103.

Held, B. S., Levine, D., & Swartz, V. (1979). Interpersonal aspects of dangerousness. *Criminal Justice & Behavior, 6*(1), 49-58.

Hindelang, M. J. (1978). Race and involvement in common law personal crimes. *American Sociological Review, 43*, 93-109.

Hochkirchen, B., & Jilek, W. (1985). Psychological dimensions of suicide and parasuicide in the Amerindians of the Pacific Northwest. *Journal of Operational Psychiatry, 16*(2), 24-28.

Holinger, P. C., & Klemen, E. H. (1982). Violent deaths in the United States, 1900-1975: Relationships between suicide, homicide, and accidental deaths. *Social Science Medicine, 16*, 1929-1938.

Holmren, C., Fitzgerald, B. J., & Carmen, R. S. (1983). Alienation and alcohol use by American Indian and Caucasian high school students. *Journal of Social Psychology, 120*, 139-140.

Hopi Health Department. (1981). *Report of the First Hopi Mental Health Conference.* Oraibi, AZ: Author.

Horwitz, A. V. (1984). The economy of social pathology. *Annual Review of Sociology, 10*(4), 95-119.

Huff-Corzine, L., Corzine, J., & Morre, D. C. (1986). Southern exposure: Deciphering the South's influence on homicide rates. *Social Forces, 64*, 906-924.

Hughes, S. P., & Dodder, D. A. (1984). Alcohol consumption patterns among American Indian and White college students. *Journal of Studies on Alcohol, 45*(5), 433-439.

Humphrey, J. A., & Kupferer, H. J. (1982). Homicide and suicide among the Cherokee and Lubee Indians of North Carolina. *International Journal of Social Psychiatry, 28*(2), 121-128.

Humphrey, J. A., & Palmer, S. (1986-87). Stressful life events and criminal homicide. *Omega, 17*(4), 127-136.

_____. (1978). Homicide and suicide in North Carolina: An emerging subculture of self-violence? In J. A. Inciardi, & A. E. Pottieger (Eds.), *Violent crime: Historical and contemporary issues.* Beverly Hills, CA: Sage.

Hunter, A. A. (1985). Doing it with numbers. *Canadian Review of Sociology & Anthropology, 22*(5), 645-672.

Iglehark, J. K. (1985). Medical care for the poor: A growing problem. *New England Journal of Medicine, 313*(1), 59-63.

Jarvis, G. K., & Boldt, M. (1982). Death styles among Canada's Indians. *Social Science Medicine, 16*, 1345-1352.

Jason, J., Strauss, L. T., & Tyler, C. W. (1983). A comparison of primary and secondary homicides in the United States. *American Journal of Epidemiology,* *117*(3), 309-313.

Jensen, G. F., Straus, J. H., & Harris, V. W. (1977). Crime, delinquency, and the American Indian. *Human Organization, 36*(3), 3.

Jilek, W., & Chunilal, R. (1976). Homicide committed by Canadian Indians and non-Indians. *International Journal of Offender Therapy & Comparative Criminology, 20*(3), 201-216.

Johnson, D. L., & Johnson, C. A. (1965). Totally discouraged: A depressive syndrome of the Dakota Sioux. *Transcultural Research, 1*(3), 141-143.

Kahane, H. (1971). *Logic and contemporary rhetoric: The use of reason in everyday life.* Belmont, CA: Wadsworth Publishing Co.

Kahn, M. W. (1982). Cultural clash and psychopathology in three aboriginal cultures. *Academic Psychology Bulletin, 4,* 553-561.

Kantor, G., & Straus, M. A. (1987). The "drunken bum" theory of wife beating. *Social Problems, 34*(3), 213-228.

Kaufman, A. (1973). Gasoline sniffing among children in a Pueblo Indian village. *Pediatrics, 51,* 1060-1064.

Kaufman, G. K., & Straus, M. A. (1987). The "drunken bum" theory of wife beating. *Social Problems, 34*(3), 214-230.

Kenen, R., & Hammerslough, C. R. (1987). Reservation and nonreservation American Indian mortality in 1970 and 1978. *Social Biology, 34*(1-2), 26-36.

Kilmas, A. (1982). *A comparison of the mortality of reservation and nonreservation Indians.* Paper presented at the annual meeting of the Population Association of America.

Kleck, G. (1979). Capital punishment, gun ownership, and homicide. *American Journal of Sociology, 84,* 882-910.

Kleck, G. (1981). Racial discrimination in criminal sentencing: A critical evaluation of the evidence with additional evidence on the death penalty. *American Sociological Review, 46*(4), 783-795.

Kleinfeld, J., & Bloom, J. (1977). Boarding schools: Effects on the mental health of Eskimo adolescents. *American Journal of Psychiatry, 134*(4), 441-447.

Komarovsky, M. (1940). *The unemployed man and his family.* New York: Dryden.

Kraus, R. F., & Buffler, P. A. (1979). Sociocultural stress and the American Native in Alaska: An analysis of changing patterns of psychiatric illness and alcohol abuse among Alaska Natives. *Culture, Medicine, and Psychiatry, 3,* 111-151.

Krush, T. P., & Bjork, J. (1965). Mental health factors in an Indian boarding school. *Mental Hygiene, 49*(1), 94-103.

Kupferer, H., & Humphrey, J. (1975). Fatal Indian violence in North Carolina. *Anthropological Quarterly, 48*(2), 236-244.

LaDuke, W., & Churchill, W. (1985). Native America: The political economy of radioactive colonialism. *Journal of Ethnic Studies, 13*(3), 107-132.

LaFromboise, T. D., & Bigfoot, D. S. (1988). Cultural and cognitive considerations in the prevention of American Indian adolescent suicide. *Journal of Adolescence, 11*(2), 139-153.

Lane, R. (1979). *Violent death in the city: Suicide, accident, and murder in 19th century Philadelphia.* Cambridge, MA: Harvard University Press.

Lefley, H. P. (1982). Self-perception and primary prevention for American

Indians. In S. M. Manson (Ed.), *New directions in prevention among American Indian and Alaska Native communities.* Portland: Oregon Health Sciences University.

Leland, J. (1976). *Fire water myths: North American Indian drinking and alcohol addiction* (Monograph No. 11). Brunswick, NJ: Rutgers Center of Alcohol Studies.

Levy, J. E. (1965). Navajo suicide. *Human Organization, 24,* 309-318.

Levy, J. E., & Kunitz, S. J. (1969). Notes on some White Mountain Apache social pathologies. *Southwestern Journal of Anthropology, 25*(2), 124-152.

_____. (1971). Indian reservations, anomie, and social pathologies. *Southwestern Journal of Anthropology, 27*(1), 97-128.

_____. 1974). *Indian drinking: Navajo practices and Anglo-American theories.* New York: Wiley-Interscience.

_____. (1987). A suicide prevention program for Hopi youth. *Social Science Medicine, 25*(8), 931-940.

Lex, B. (1987). Review of alcohol problems in ethnic minority groups. *Journal of Consulting & Clinical Psychology, 53*(3), 293-300.

Linton, R. (1972). The distinctive aspects of acculturation. In D. W. Walker (Ed.), *The emergent Native Americans: A reader in culture contact.* Boston, MA: Little, Brown and Co.

Loftin, C., & Hill, R. H. (1974). Regional subculture and homicide. *American Sociological Review, 39,* 714-724.

Loftin, C., & Parker, R. N. (1985). An errors-in-model of the effect of poverty on urban homicide rates. *Criminology, 23,* 269-279.

Luebben, R. A. (1964). Anglo law and Navajo behavior. *Kiva, 29*(3), 60-75.

MacAndrew, C., & Edgerton, R. B. (1970). *Drunken comportment: A social explanation.* London: Thomas Nelson & Sons.

May, P. A. (1975). Arrests, alcohol and alcohol legalization. *Plains Anthropologist, 20,* 129-134.

_____. (1977). Explanations of Native American drinking: A literature review. *Plains Anthropologist, 22*(77), 223-232.

_____. (1982a). Substance abuse and American Indians: Prevalence and susceptibility. *International Journal of the Addictions, 17*(1), 1185-1209.

_____. (1982b). Contemporary crime and the American Indian: A survey and analysis of the literature. *Plains Anthropologist,* 125-138.

_____. (1986). Alcohol and drug misuse prevention programs for American Indians: Needs and opportunities. *Journal of Studies on Alcohol, 47*(3), 189-195.

_____. (1989). Alcohol abuse and alcoholism among American Indians: An overview. In T. D. Watts & R. Wright, Jr. (Eds.), *Alcoholism in minority populations.* Springfield, IL: Charles C. Thomas.

May, P. A., & Dizmang, L. A. (1974). Suicide and the American Indian. *Psychiatric Annals, 4*(2), 22-28.

Maynard, E., & Twiss, G. (1970). *That these people may live.* Washington, DC: U.S. Government Printing Office.

McCord, J., McCord, W., & Thurber, W. (1962). Some effects of paternal absence on male children. *Journal of Abnormal & Social Psychology, 64,* 361-369.

McIntosh, J. L. (1980-81). Suicide among Native Americans: A compilation of findings. *Omega, 11*(1), 303-316.

_____. (1983-84). Suicide among Native American Indians: Further tribal data and considerations. *Omega, 14*(3), 215-229.

McShane, D. (1988). An analysis of mental health research with American Indian youth. *Journal of Adolescence, 11*, 87-116.

Medicine, B. (1981). Native American resistance to integration: Contemporary confrontations and religious revitalization. *Plains Anthropologist, 94*, 277-286.

Merton, R. K. (1968). *Social theory and social structure.* Glencoe, IL: Free Press.

Messner, S. F. (1982). Poverty, inequality and the urban homicide rate. *Criminology, 20*(2), 103-114.

_____. (1983a). Regional and racial effects on the urban homicide rate: The subculture of violence revisited. *American Journal of Sociology, 88*, 997-1007.

_____. (1983b). Regional differences in the economic correlates of urban homicide rates. *Criminology, 21*, 477-488.

Mesteth, L. (1968). Gas and glue sniffing among the school age population. *Pine Ridge Research Bulletin, 4*, 36-40.

Miller, W. B. (1958). Lower-class culture as a generating milieu of gang delinquency. *Journal of Social Issues, 14*, 5-19.

Mindell, C., & Gurwitt, A. (1977). The placement of American Indian children: The need for change. In S. Unger (Ed.), *The destruction of the American family.* New York: Association on American Indian Affairs.

Minnis, M. S. (1963). The relationship of the social structure of an Indian community to adult and juvenile delinquency. *Social Forces, 41*, 395-403.

Mintz, S., & Kellog, S. (1988). *Domestic revolutions, in a social history of American family life.* Glencoe, IL: Free Press.

Mitchell, W., & Patch, K. (1981). Indian alcoholism and education. *Journal of American Indian Education, 21*, 31-33.

Mooney, J. (1900). *Myths of the Cherokee* (19th Annual Report). Washington, DC: Bureau of American Ethnology.

Morinins, E. A. (1982). "Getting Straight": Behavioral patterns in a skid row Indian community. *Urban Anthropology, 11*(2), 193-212.

Motto, J. A. (1984). Assessment of suicide risk. *Medical Aspects of Human Sexuality, 18*(10), 134.

Mucha, J. (1984). American Indian success in the urban setting. *Urban Anthropologist, 13*(4), 329-354.

Murphy, S. P. (1974). Emergency medical care: A right or a dream. In C. W. Sproul & P. J. Mullanney (Eds.), *Emergency care: Assessment and intervention.* St. Louis: C. V. Mosby.

National Center for Education Statistics. (1979). *The condition of education.* Washington, DC: Author.

Navajo Health Authority. (1979). *The Navajo Alcohol Abuse and Education Project: Final report—Programs needs, recommendation and alcoholism treatment model.* Window Rock, AZ: Navajo Health Authority.

Nebraska Advisory Committee to the U.S. Commission on Civil Rights. (1974). *Inmate rights and institutional response: The Nebraska State Prison System.*

New York Times. (1991, March 5). Census finds many claiming new identity: Indian, p. 1, col. 3.

Norman, J. (1969). *Medicine in the ghetto.* New York: Appleton-Century-Crofts.

Oetting, E. R., Edwards, R., Goldstein, G.S., & Garic-Mason, V. (1980). Drug use among adolescents of five southwestern Native American Indian tribes. *International Journal of the Addictions, 15*(3), 439-445.

Ogden, M., Spector, M. I., & Hill, C., Jr. (1970). Suicides and homicides among Indians. *Public Health Reports, 85*(2), 75-80.

Orubuloye, I. D., & Cladwell, J. C. (1975). The impact of public health services on mortality. *Population Studies, 29,* 259-272.

Page, V. (1985). Reservation development in the United States: Peripherality in the core. *American Indian Culture & Research Journal, 9*(3), 21-35.

Palmer, S. H. (1972). *The violent society.* New Haven, CT: Yale University Press.

Palmer, S. H., & Humphrey, J. A. (1978). Offender-victim relationships in criminal homicide followed by offender's suicide, North Carolina, 1972-1977. *Suicide and Life-Threatening Behavior, 10,* 106-118.

Park, R., & Burgess, E. W. (1921). *Introduction to the science of sociology.* Chicago, IL: University of Chicago Press.

Parker, R. N., & Loftin, C. (1985). The effect of poverty on urban homicide rates: An error-in-variable model. *Criminology, 23,* 269-287.

Parrillo, V. N. (1985). *Strangers to these shores: Race and ethnic relations in the United States.* New York: John Wiley.

Peters, R. (1981). Suicidal behavior among Native Americans: An annotated bibliography. *White Cloud Journal, 2*(3), 9-19.

Pfeffer, C. R. (1986). *The suicidal child.* New York: Guilford Press.

Pfeffer, C. R., Zuckerman, S., Plutchick, R., & Mizruchi, M. S. (1984). Suicidal behavior of normal school children: A comparison with child psychiatric inpatients. *Journal of the American Academy of Child Psychiatry, 23,* 416-423.

Quinney, R. (1979). *Criminology* (2nd ed.). Boston: Little, Brown.

Radelet, M. L. (1981). Racial characteristics and the imposition of the death penalty. *American Sociological Review, 46,* 918-927.

Randall, A., & Randall, B. (1978). Criminal justice and the American Indian. *Indian Historian, 11*(2), 42-48.

Rapid City Journal. (1990, June 7). American Indians gather to save language, culture, col. 1, B3.

Raymond, M. P., & Raymond, E. V. (1984). *Identification and assessment of model Indian Health Service alcoholism projects.* Minneapolis: First Phoenix American Corp.

Reasons, C. (1972). Crime and the American Indian. In H. Bahr, B. Chadwick, & S. Day (Eds.), *Native Americans today: Sociological perspectives.* New York: Harper and Row.

Red Horse, Y. (1982). A cultural network model: Perspectives for adolescent services and paraprofessional training. In S. M. Manson (Ed.), *New directions in prevention among American Indian and Alaska Native communities.* Portland: Oregon Health Sciences University.

Reed, J. S. (1971). To live and die in Dixie: A contribution to the study of southern violence. *Political Science Quarterly, 86,* 429-443.

Resnik, H.L.P., & Dizmang, L. H. (1971). Observations on suicidal behavior among American Indians. *American Journal of Psychiatry, 127*(7), 882-887.

Riffenburgh, A. S. (1964). Cultural influences and crime among Indian-Americans of the Southwest. *Federal Probation, 23*(1), 63-66.

Riner, R. D. (1979). American Indian education: A rite that fails. *Anthropology & Education Quarterly, 10*, 236-253.

Rosenbaum, A., & O'Leary, K. D. (1981). Marital violence: Characteristics of abusive couples. *Journal of Consulting and Clinical Psychology, 49*, 63-71.

Rouse, L. P., & Hanson, J. R. (1990). *Attitudes toward American Indians: Implications for teaching about minorities.* Paper presented at the annual meeting of the Society for the Study of Social Problems, Washington, DC.

Rowles, G. D., & Reinharz, S. (Eds.) (1988). Qualitative gerontology: Themes and challenges. In *Qualitative gerontology.* New York: Springer Publishing.

Ryan, R. A., & Spence, J. D. (1978). American Indian mental health research: Local control and cultural sensitivity. *White Cloud Journal, 1*(1), 15-18.

Sampson, R. J. (1985). Race and criminal violence: A demographically disaggregated analysis of urban homicide. *Crime & Delinquency, 31*(1), 47-82.

Schottstaedt, M. F., & Bjork, J. (1977). Inhalant abuse in an Indian boarding school. *American Journal of Psychiatry, 134*, 1290-1293.

Schur, E. M. (1971). *Labeling deviant behavior: Its sociological implications.* New York: Harper & Row.

Scott, W. J. (1986). Attachment to Indian culture and the "difficult situation": A study of American Indian college students. *Youth & Society, 17*(4), 381-395.

Sellin, T. (1983). *Culture, conflict, and crime.* New York: Social Science Research Council.

Shafi, M., Carrigan, S., Whittinghill, J. R., & Derrick, A. (1985). Psychological autopsy of completed suicide in children and adolescents. *American Journal of Psychiatry, 142*(9), 1061-1064.

Shaw, C. R., & McKay, H. D. (1969). *Juvenile delinquency and urban areas.* Chicago: University of Chicago Press.

Sheehan, B. (1980). *Savagism and civility: Indians and Englishmen in colonial Virginia.* Cambridge: Cambridge University Press.

Shore, J. H. (1969). *Suicide and suicide attempts among American Indians of the Pacific Northwest.* (Indian Health Service, Room 200, 921 SW Washington, Portland, OR 97205.)

Shore, J. H., & Manson, S. M. (1981). Cross-cultural studies of depression among American Indians and Alaska natives. *White Cloud Journal, 2*(2), 5-12.

Shupe, L. M. (1954). Alcohol, crime, a study of the urine alcohol concentration found in 882 persons during or immediately after the commission of a felony. *Policy Sciences, 44*, 661-664.

Silberman, C. E. (1987). *Criminal violence, criminal justice.* New York: Random House.

Skogan, W. G. (1989). Social change and the future of violent crime. In T. R. Gurr (Ed.), *Violence in America: The history of crime.* Newbury Park, CA: Sage Publications.

Smith, M. W., & Parker, R. N. (1980). Type of homicide and variation in regional rates. *Social Forces, 59*(1), 136-147.

Snipp, C. M. & Summers, G. F. (1991). American Indians and economic poverty. In Cynthia Duncan (Ed.), *Rural poverty in America*. Westport, CT: Auburn House.

Sorkin, A. L. (1976). The economic and social status of the American Indian, 1940-1970. *Journal of Negro Education, 45*(4), 432-447.

———. (1978) *The urban American Indian*. Lexington, MA: D. C. Heath.

South, S. J., & Cohen, L. E. (1985). Unemployment and the homicide rate: A paradox resolved? *Social Indicators Research, 17*, 325-343.

Spaulding, J. M. (1985-86). Recent suicide rates among ten Ojibwa Indian bands in Northwestern Ontario. *Omega, 16*(4), 347-354.

Spector, P. E. (1975). Population density and unemployment: The effects on the incidence of violent crime in the American city. *Criminology, 12*, 399-401.

Staus, J. H. (1976). The study of American families: Implications of applied research. *Family Perspective, 20*(4), 337-349.

Staus, J. H., Chadwick, B., Bahr, H. M., & Halverson, L. K. (1979). An experimental outreach legal aid program for an urban Native American population utilizing legal paraprofessionals. *Human Organization, 38*(4), 386-393.

Stets, J. E., & Straus, M. A. (1990). The marriage license as a hitting license: A comparison of assaults in dating, cohabiting and married couples. In M. A. Straus, & R. J. Gelles (Eds.), *Physical violence in American families*. New Brunswick, NJ: Transaction Publishers.

Stewart, O. (1964). Questions regarding American Indian criminality. *Human Organization, 23*(1), 61-66.

Straus, M. A. (1985). *The validity of U.S. states as units for sociological research*. Paper presented at the annual meeting of the American Sociological Association, Washington, DC.

———. (1990). Social Stress and marital violence in a national sample of American families. In M. A. Straus, & R. J. Gelles (Eds.), *Physical violence in American families*. New Brunswick, NJ: Transaction Publishers.

Straus, M. A., & Gelles, R. J. (Eds.) (1990). *Physical violence in American families*, New Brunswick, NJ: Transaction Publishers.

Straus, M. A., Gelles, R. J., & Steinmetz, S. K. (1980). *Behind closed doors*. Garden City, NY: Anchor.

Suitor, J. J., Pillemer, K., & Straus, M. A. (1990). Marital violence in a life course perspective. In M. A. Straus & R. J. Gelles (Eds.), *Physical violence in American families*. New Brunswick, NJ: Transaction Publishers.

Sviridoff, M., & Thompson, J. W. (1979). *Linkages between employment and crime: A qualitative study of Rikers releases*. New York: Vera Institute of Justice.

Swanson, D. W., Bratrude, A. P., & Brown, E. M. (1971). Alcohol abuse in a population of Indian children. *Diseases of the Nervous System, 32*, 835-842.

Swigert, V. L., & Farrell, R. A. (1977). Normal homicides and the law. *American Sociological Review, 42*, 16-32.

Thomas, J. (1987). Inhalant use among American Indian youth. *Child Psychiatry & Human Development, 18*(1), 36-46.

Thomas, W. I., & Znaniecki, F. (1920). *The Polish peasant in Europe and America*. Chicago, IL: The University of Chicago Press.

Tippeconnic, J. W. (1988). A survey: Attitudes toward the education of American Indians. *Journal of American Indian Education, 28*(1), 34-36.

Topper, M. D. (1974). Navajo "alcoholism," drinking, alcohol abuse, and treatment in a changing cultural environment. In J. C. Weibel-Orlando (Ed.), *Indians, ethnicity and alcohol.*

Townsley, H. C. & Goldstein, G. S. (1977). One view of the etiology of depression in the American Indian. *Public Health Reports, 92*(5), 458-461.

Unger, S. (Ed.). (1977). *The destruction of American Indian families.* New York: Association on American Indian Affairs.

U.S. Bureau of the Census. (1980). *American Indians, subject report* (Census of the Population Report No. PC21F). Washington, DC: U.S. Department of Commerce.

U.S. Congress, Office of Technology Assessment. (1990). *Indian adolescent mental health.* Washington, DC: U.S. Government Printing Office.

U.S. Department of Health and Human Services. (1981). *Report of the Third National Indian Child Conference: The Indian family—Foundations for the future.* Albuquerque: Indian Health Service, Office of Mental Health Programs.

U.S. Department of Health and Human Services. (1983). *Report of the Fifth National Indian Child Conference: Save the Children Committee.* Albuquerque: Indian Health Service, Office of Mental Health Programs.

U.S. Department of Justice, Federal Bureau of Investigation. (1990). *Uniform Crime Reports.* Washington, DC: U.S. Government Printing Office.

Vizenor, G. (1986-87). American Indians and drunkenness. *Journal of Ethical Studies, 11*(4), 83-87.

Wallace, H. M. (1972). The health of American Indian children. *Health Services Report, 87,* 867-876.

Web, J. P., & Willard W. (1975). Six American Indian patterns of suicide. In N. L. Farberow (Ed.), *Suicide in different cultures.* Baltimore, MD: University Park Press.

Weibel-Orlando, J. C. (1974). Ethnic self and alcohol use. In J. C. Weibel-Orlando (Ed.), *Indians, ethnicity and alcohol.*

Weisner, T. S., Weibel-Orlando, J. C., & Long, L. (1984). Serious drinking, White man's drinking and teetotaling: Drinking levels and styles in an urban American Indian population. *Journal of Studies on Alcohol, 45*(3), 237-250.

Westermeyer, J., & Brantner, J. (1972). Violent death and alcohol use among the Chippewa in Minnesota. *Minnesota Medicine, 55,* 749-752.

Westermeyer, J., & Neider, J. (1985). Cultural affiliation among American Indian alcoholics: Correlations and change over a ten year period. *Journal of Operational Psychiatry, 16,* 17-23.

Westlake Van Winkle, N., & May, P. A. (1986). Native American suicide in New Mexico, 1957-1979: A comparative study. *Human Organization, 45*(4), 296-309.

Weyler, R. (1984). *Blood of the land: The government and corporate war against the American Indian movement.* New York: Vintage Books.

White, R. H. (1990). Tribal assets: The rebirth of Native America. New York: Henry Holt.

Whittaker, J. O. (1982). Alcohol and the Standing Rock Sioux Tribe: A twenty year follow-up study. *Journal of Studies on Alcohol, 43*(3), 191-200.

Wilkinson, K. P. (1984). A research note on homicide and rurality. *Social Forces, 63*, 445-452.

Willard,. W. (1979). American indians. In L. D. Hankoff, & B. Eihsidler (Eds.), *Suicide*. New York: PSG Publishing Co.

Williams, K. R. (1984). Economic sources of homicide: Reestimating the effects of poverty and inequality. *American Sociological Review, 49*(2), 283-289.

Williams, K. R., & Bachman, R. (1988). *Examining the impact of medical resource availability on weapon-specific homicides*. Paper presented at the 1988 meeting of the American Society of Criminology, Montreal.

Williams, K. R., & Flewelling, R. L. (1987). Family, acquaintance, and stranger homicide: Alternative procedures for rate calculations. *Criminology, 25*(3), 543-560.

———. (1988). The social production of criminal homicide: A comparative study of disaggregated rates in American cities. *American Sociological Review, 53*(3), 421-431.

Williams, L. E. (1979). *Antecedents of urban Indian crime*. Unpublished doctoral dissertation. Brigham Young University, Provo, Utah.

———. (1981). *Native Americans and the criminal justice system: Equal justice for all?* Unpublished manuscript. (Midwestern State University, Wichita Falls, TX.)

Wilson, J. Q., & Cook, P. J. (1985). Unemployment and crime—What is the connection? *Public Interest, 79*(1), 3-8.

Wilson, T. P. (1986). Qualitative versus quantitative methods in social research. *Bulletin on Methodological Sociology, 10*, 25-51.

Winfree, T. L., & Griffiths, C. T. (1975). An examination of factors related to the parole survival of American Indians. Unpublished manuscript.

Wolfgang, M. E. (1958). *Patterns of criminal homicide*. Philadelphia: University of Pennsylvania Press.

———. (1967). *The subculture of violence*. Beverly Hills, CA: Sage.

Wolfgang, M. E., & Ferracuti, F. (1967). *The subculture of violence*. Newbury Park, CA: Sage Publications.

Wright, J. L., Jr. (1981). *The only land they knew: The tragic story of the American Indians in the Old South*. New York: Free Press.

Young, T. J. (1988). Substance use and abuse among Native Americans. *Clinical Psychology Review, 18*, 125-138.

Young, T. J., LaPlante, C., & Robbins, W. (1987). Indians before the law: An assessment of contravening cultural/legal ideologies. *Quarterly Journal of Ideology, 11*, 59-70.

Zelditch, M., Jr. (1962). Some methodological problems of field studies. *American Journal of Sociology, 67*.

Index

About the Author

RONET BACHMAN is a Research Analyst and Statistician with the Bureau of Justice Statistics, U.S. Justice Department. She is also Visiting Assistant Professor of Criminal Justice and Criminology at the University of Maryland.